The New Nihilism

The New Nihilism

Peter Lamborn Wilson

Bottle of Smoke Press
New York

Acknowledgments:

The title essay was published as a pamphlet by Enemy Combatant (EC Publications, Box 1014, Jacksonville, OR 97530).

Thanx to editors Raymond Foye, Charles Stein, & Bill Roberts.

FIRST EDITION

ISBN-13:   978-1-937073-72-5

Library of Congress Cataloging-in-Publication data has been applied for.

Bottle of Smoke Press
29 Sugar Hill Road
North Salem, NY 10560

www.bospress.net

CONTENTS

For Mick Taussig

The New Nihilism

It feels increasingly difficult to tell the difference between — on one hand — being old, sick, and defeated, and — on the other hand — living in a time-&-place that is itself senile, tired, and defeated. Sometimes I think it's just me — but then I find that even some younger, healthier people seem to be undergoing similar sensations of ennui, despair, and impotent anger. Maybe it's not just me.

A friend of mine attributed the general turn to disillusion with "everything", including old-fashioned radical/activist positions, to disappointment over the last political regime in the US, which was somehow expected to usher in a turn away from the reactionary decades since the 1980s, or even a "progress" toward some sort of democratic socialism. Although I myself didn't share this optimism (I always assume that anyone who even *wants* to be President of the US must be a psychopathic murderer) I can see that "youth" suffered a powerful disillusionment at the utter failure of Liberalism to turn the tide against Capitalist Triumphalism. The disillusionment gave rise to OCCUPY WALL ST. and the failure of OCCUPY led to a move toward sheer negation.

However I think this merely political analysis of the "new nothing" may be too two-dimensional to do justice to the extent to which all hope of "change" has died under Kognitive Kapital and the technopathocracy. Despite my remnant hippy flower-power sentiments I too feel this "terminal" condition (as Nietzsche called it), which I express by saying, only half-jokingly, that we have at last reached the Future, and that the truly horrible truth of the End of the World is that it doesn't end.

One big J.G. Ballard/Philip K. Dick online shopping mall from now till eternity basically.

This IS the future — how do you like it so far? Life in the Ruins: not so bad for the bourgeoisie, the loyal servants of the One Percent. Air-conditioned ruins! No Ragnarök, no Rapture, no dramatic closure: just an endless re-run of reality TV cop shows. 2012 has come and gone, and we're still in debt to some faceless bank, still chained to our screens.

Most people — in order to live at all — seem to need around themselves a penumbra of "illusion" (to quote Nietzsche again): — that the world is just rolling along as usual, some good days some bad, but in essence no different now than in 10,000 BC or 1492 AD or next year. Some even need to believe in Progress, that the Future will solve all our problems, and even that life is much better for us now than for (say) people in the 5ᵗʰ century AD. We live longer thanx to Modern Science — of course our extra years are largely spent as "medical objects" — sick and worn out but kept ticking by Machines & Pills that spin huge profits for a few mega-corporations & insurance companies. Nation of Struldbrugs.

True, we're suffocating in the mire generated by our rule of sick machines under the Numisphere of Money. At least ten times as much money now exists than it would take to buy the whole world — and yet species are vanishing, space itself is vanishing, ice-caps melting, air and water grown toxic, culture grown toxic, landscape sacrificed to agribusiness and megamalls, noise-fascism, etc., etc. But Science will cure all ills that Science has created — in the Future (in the "long run", when we're all dead, as Lord Keynes put it); so meanwhile we'll carry on consuming the world and shitting it out as waste — because it's convenient and efficient and profitable to do so, and because *we like it*.

Well, this is all a bunch of whiney left-liberal clichés, no? Heard it before a million times. Yawn. How boring, how infantile, how useless. Even if it were all true . . . what can we do about it? If our Anointed Leaders can't or won't stop it, who will? God? Satan? The "People"?

All the fashionable "solutions" to the "crisis", from electronic democracy to revolutionary violence, from locavorism to solar-powered dingbats, from financial market regulation to the General Strike — all of them, however ridiculous or sublime, depend on one preliminary radical change — a seismic shift in human consciousness. Without such a change all hope of reform is futile. And if such a change were somehow to occur, no "reform" would be necessary. The world would simply change. The whales would be saved. War no more. And so on.

What force could (even in theory) bring about such a shift? Religion? In 6,000 years of organized religion matters have only gotten worse. Psychedelic drugs in the reservoirs? The Mayan calendar? Nostalgia? Terror?

If catastrophic disaster is now inevitable, perhaps the "Survivalist prepper" scenario will ensue, and a few brave millions will create a green utopia in the smoking waste. But won't Capitalism find a way to profit even from the End of the World? Some would claim that it's doing so already. The true catastrophe may be the final apotheosis of commodity fetishism.

Let's assume for the sake of argument that this paradise of power tools and back-up alarms is all we've got & all we're going to get. Capitalism can deal with global warming — it can sell water-wings and disaster insurance. So it's all over, let's say — but we've still got television & Twitter. Childhood's End — i.e. the child as ultimate consumer, eager for the brand. Terrorism or home shopping network — take yr pick (democracy means *choice*).

Since the death of the Historical Movement of the Social in 1989 (last gasp of the hideous "short" XXth century that started in 1914) the only "alternative" to Capitalist Neo-Liberal totalitarianism that seems to have emerged is religious neo-fascism. I understand *why* someone would want to be a violent fundamentalist bigot — I sympathize — but just because I feel sorry for lepers doesn't mean I want to be one.

When I attempt to retain some shreds of my former anti-pessimism I fantasize that History may not be over, that some sort of Populist Green Social Democracy might yet emerge to challenge the obscene smugness of "Money Interests" — something along the lines of 1970s Scandinavian monarcho-socialism — which in retrospect now looks like the most humane form of the State ever to have emerged from the putrid suck-hole of Civilization. (Think of Amsterdam in its hey-day.) Of course as an anarchist I'd still have to oppose it — but at least I'd have the luxury of believing that, in such a situation, anarchy might actually stand some chance of success. Even if such a movement were to emerge, however, we can rest damn-well assured it won't happen in the USA. Or anywhere in the ghost-realm of dead Marxism, either. Maybe Scotland?

It would seem quite pointless to wait around for such a rebirth of the Social. Years ago many radicals gave up all hope of The Revolution, and the few who still adhere to it remind me of religious fanatics. It might be soothing to lapse into such doctrinaire revolutionism, just as it might be soothing to sink into mystical religion — but for me at least both options have lost their savor. Again, I sympathize with those true believers (although not so much when they lapse into authoritarian leftism or fascism) — nevertheless, frankly, I'm too depressed to embrace their illusions.

If the End-Time scenario sketched above be considered actually true, what alternatives might exist besides suicidal despair? After much thought I've come up with three basic strategies.

1) Passive Escapism. Keep your head down, don't make waves. Capitalism permits all sorts of "life-styles" (I hate that word) — just pick one & try to enjoy it. You're even allowed to live as a dirt farmer without electricity & infernal combustion, like a sort of secular Amish refusenik. Well, maybe not. But at least you could *flirt* with such a life. "Smoke Pot, Eat Chicken, Drink Tea", as we used to say in the 60s in the Moorish Orthodox Church of America, our psychedelic cult. Hope they don't catch you. Fit yourself into some Permitted Category such as Neo-Hippy or even Anabaptist.

2) Active escapism. In this scenario you attempt to create the optimal conditions for the emergence of Autonomous Zones, whether temporary, periodic or even (semi)permanent. In 1984 when I first coined the term Temporary Autonomous Zone (TAZ) I envisioned it as a complement to The Revolution — although I was already, to be truthful, tired of waiting for a moment that seemed to have failed in 1968. The TAZ would give a taste or premonition of real *liberties*: in effect you would attempt to live *as if* the Revolution had already occurred, so as not to die without ever having experienced "free freedom" (as Rimbaud called it, *liberté libre*). Create your own pirate utopia.

Of course the TAZ can be as brief & simple as a really good dinner party, but the true autonomist will want to maximize the potential for longer & deeper experiences of authentic lived life. Almost inevitably this will involve *crime,* so it's necessary to think like a criminal, not a victim. A "Johnson" as Burroughs used to say — not a "mark". How else can one live (and live well) without Work? Work, the curse of the thinking class. Wage slavery. If you're lucky enough to be a successful artist, you can perhaps achieve relative autonomy without breaking any obvious laws (except the laws of good taste, perhaps). Or you could inherit a million. (More than a million would be a curse.) Forget revolutionary morality — the question is, can you *afford* your taste of freedom? For most of us, crime will be not only a pleasure but a necessity. The old anarcho-Illegalists showed the way: individual expropriation . Getting caught of course spoils the whole thing — but *risk* is an aspect of self-authenticity.

One scenario I've imagined for active Escapism would be to move to a remote rural area along with several hundred other libertarian socialists — enough to take over the local government (municipal or even county) and elect or control the sheriffs & judges, the parent/teacher association, volunteer fire department and even the water authority. Fund the venture with cultivation of illegal *phantastica* and carry on a discreet trade. Organize as a "Union of Egoists" for mutual benefit & ecstatic pleasures — perhaps under the guise of "communes" or even monasteries, who cares. Enjoy it as long as it lasts.

I know for a fact that this plan is being worked on in several places in America — but of course I'm not going to say *where.*

Another possible model for individual escapists might be the *nomadic adventurer.* Given that the whole world seems to be turning into a giant parking lot or social media network, I don't know if this option remains open, but I suspect that it might. The trick would be to travel in places where tourists don't — if such places still exist — and to involve oneself in fascinating and dangerous situations. For example if I were young and healthy I'd've gone to France to take part in the TAZ that grew around resistance to the new airport — or to Greece — or Mexico — wherever the perverse spirit of rebellion crops up. The problem here is of course funding. (Sending back statues stuffed with hash is no longer a good idea.) How to pay for yr life of adventure? Love will find a way. It doesn't matter so much if one agrees with the ideals of Tahrir Square or Zuccotti Park — the point is just to *be there*.

3) Revenge. I call it *Zarathustra's Revenge* because as Nietzsche said, revenge may be second rate but it's not nothing. One might enjoy the satisfaction of terrifying the bastards for at least a few moments. Formerly I advocated "Poetic Terrorism", rather than actual violence, the idea being that art could be wielded as a weapon. Now I've come to doubt it. But perhaps weapons might be wielded as art. From the sledgehammer of the Luddites to the black bomb of the attentat, destruction could serve as a form of creativity, for its own sake, or for purely æsthetic reasons, without any illusions about revolution. Oscar Wilde meets the *acte gratuit*: a dandyism of despair.

What troubles me about this idea is that it seems impossible to distinguish here between the action of post-leftist anarcho-nihilists and the action of post-rightist neo-traditionalist reactionaries. For that matter, a bomb may as well be detonated by fundamentalist fanatics — what difference would it make to the victims or the "innocent bystanders"? Blowing up a nanotechnology lab — why shouldn't this be the act of a desperate monarchist as easily as that of a Nietzschean anarchist?

In a recent book by Tiqqun *(Theory of Bloom)*, it was fascinating to come suddenly across the constellation of Nietzsche, René Guénon, Julius Evola, *et al.* as examples of a sharp and just critique of the Bloom syndrome — i.e., of progress-as-illusion. Of course the "beyond left and right" position has two sides — one approaching from the left, the other from the right. The European New Right (Alain de Benoist & his gang) are big admirers of Guy Debord, for a similar reason (his critique, not his proposals). The post-left can now appreciate Traditionalism as a reaction against modernity just as the neo-traditionalists can appreciate Situationism. But this doesn't mean that post-anarchism anarchists are identical with post-fascism fascists.

I'm reminded of the situation in fin-de-siècle France that gave rise to a strange alliance between anarchists and monarchists; for example the *Cercle Proudhon*. This surreal conjunction came about for two reasons: a) both factions hated liberal democracy, and b) the monarchists had money. The marriage gave birth to weird progeny, such as Georges Sorel. And Mussolini famously began his career as an Individualist anarchist.

Another link between left & right could be analyzed as a kind of existentialism; once again Nietzsche is the founding parent here, I think. On the left there were thinkers like Gide and Camus. On the right, that illuminated villain Baron Julius Evola used to tell his little ultra-right groupuscules in Rome to attack the Modern World — even though the restoration of tradition was a hopeless dream — if only as an act of magical self-creation. Being trumps essence. One must cherish no attachment to mere *results*. Surely Tiqqun's advocacy of the "perfect Surrealist act" (firing a revolver at random into a crowd of "innocent bystanders") partakes of this form of *action-as-despair*. (Incidentally I have to confess that this sort of thing has always — to my regret — prevented my embracing Surrealism: it's just too cruel. I don't admire de Sade either.)

Of course, as we know, the problem with the Traditionalists is that they were never traditional enough. They looked back at a lost civilization as their "goal" (religion, mysticism, mònarchism, arts-&-crafts, etc.) whereas they should have realized that the *real* tradition is the "primordial anarchy" of the Stone Age, tribalism, hunting/gathering, animism — what I call the Neanderthal Liberation Front. Paul Goodman used the term "Neolithic Conservatism" to describe his brand of anarchism — but "Paleolithic Reaction" might be more appropriate.

The other major problem with the Traditionalist Right is that the entire emotional tone of the movement is rooted in self-repression. Here a rough Reichean analysis suffices to demonstrate that the authoritarian body reflects a damaged soul, and that only anarchy is compatible with real self-realization. Maybe.

The European New Right that arose in the '90s still carries on its propaganda — and these chaps are not just vulgar nationalist chauvinist anti-Semite homophobic thugs—they're intellectuals & artists. I think they're *evil,* but that doesn't mean I find them boring. Or even *wrong* on certain points. They also hate the nanotechnologists!

Although I attempted to set off a few bombs in the 1960s (against the war in Vietnam) I'm glad, on the whole, that they failed to detonate (technology was never my *métier*). It saves me from wondering if I would've experienced "moral qualms". Instead I chose the path of propagandist and remained an activist in anarchist media from 1984 to about 2004. I collaborated with the Autonomedia publishing collective, the IWW, the John Henry Mackay Society (Left Stirnerites) and the old NYC Libertarian Book Club (founded by comrades of Emma Goldman, some of whom I knew, & who are now all dead). I had a radio show on WBAI (Pacifica) for 18 years. I lectured all over Europe and East Europe in the '90s. I had a very nice time, thank you. But anarchism seems even further off now than it looked in 1984, or indeed 1958, when I first became an anarchist by reading George Harriman's *Krazy Kat.* Well, being an existentialist means you never have to say you're sorry.

In the last few years in anarchist circles there's been a trend "back" to Stirner/Nietzsche Individualism — because after all, who can take revolutionary anarcho-communism or syndicalism seriously anymore? Since I've adhered to this Individualist position for decades (although tempered by admiration for Charles Fourier and certain "spiritual anarchists" like Gustav Landauer) I naturally find this trend agreeable.

"Green anarchists" & Anti-Civilization Neo-primitivists seem (some of them) to be moving toward a new pole of attraction, *nihilism.* Perhaps neo-nihilism would serve as a better label, since this tendency is not simply replicating the nihilism of Russian *narodniks* or the French attentatists of circa 1890 to 1912, however much the new nihilists look to the old ones as precursors. I share their *critique* — in fact I think I have been mirroring it to a large extent in this essay: creative despair, let's call it. What

I do not understand is their *proposal* — if any. "What is to be done?" was originally a nihilist slogan, after all, before Lenin appropriated it. I presume that my option #1, passive escape, would not suit the agenda. As for Active Escapism, to use the suffix "ism" implies some form not only of ideology but also some *action*. What is the logical outcome of this train of thought?

As an animist I experience the world (outside Civilization) as essentially sentient. The death of God means the rebirth of the gods, as Nietzsche implied in his last "mad" letters from Turin — the resurrection of the great god PAN — Chaos, Eros, Gaia, & Old Night, as Hesiod put it — Ontological anarchy, Desire, Life itself, & the Darkness of revolt & negation — all seem to me as real as they need to be.

I still adhere to a certain kind of spiritual anarchism — but only as heresy and paganism, not as orthodoxy and monotheism. I have great respect for Dorothy Day — her writing influenced me in the '60s — and Ivan Illich, whom I knew personally — but in the end I cannot deal with the cognitive dissonance between anarchism and the Pope. Nevertheless I can believe in the *re-paganization of monotheism*. I hold to this pagan tradition because I sense the universe as alive, not as "dead matter". As a life-long psychedelicist I have always thought that matter & spirit are identical, and that this fact alone legitimizes what Theory calls "desire".

From this p.o.v. the phrase "revolution of everyday life" still seems to have some validity — if only in terms of the second proposal, Active Escapism or the TAZ. As for the third possibility — Zarathustra's revenge — this seems like a possible path for the new nihilism, at least from a philosophical perspective. But since I am unable personally to advocate it, I leave the question open.

But here — I think — is the point at which I both meet with & diverge from the new nihilism. I too seem to believe that Predatory Capitalism has won and that no revolution is possible in the classical sense of that term. But somehow I can't bring myself to be "against everything". Within the Temporary Autonomous Zone there still seems to persist the possibility of "authentic life", if only for a moment — and if this position amounts to mere Escapism, then let us become Houdini. The new surge of interest in Individualism is obviously a response to the Death of the Social. But does the new nihilism imply the death even of the individual and the "union of egoists" or Nietzschean free spirits? On my good days, I like to think not.

No matter which of the three paths one takes (or others I can't imagine) it seems to me that the essential thing is not to collapse into mere apathy. Depression we may have to accept, impotent rage we may have to accept, revolutionary pessimism we may have to accept. But as e.e. cummings (anarchist poet) said, "there is some shit we will not eat" lest we simply become the enemy by default. Can't go on, must go on. Cultivate rosebuds, even selfish pleasures, as long as a few birds & flowers still remain. Even love may not be impossible.

July 2014

Comix

It would be nice if Americans could take pride in the real donations we've made to the possibility of an unshadowed joy of life in the world. Instead of boasting about our "freedom", which was founded on the oppression of slaves and Indians, or our conquests, our power, our particularist virtues — which are based on war (mass murder) and the repression of our own soul life by Puritanism and Work — wouldn't it feel refreshing to take seriously for once some of our actual acts of genius and grace?

Jazz, which is really the only serious form of music to be invented in America, seems to have been eclipsed since its heyday in the 1940s and 50s by the triumph of lousy pop schlock that provides the universal public soundtrack for our present ecstatic Capitalism. It doesn't seem at all inappropriate to me to compare — favorably — the art of Bird, Thelonious, Coltrane or Cecil Taylor with that of Satie, Stravinsky, Prokofiev or Charles Ives. But you will never hear Monk's "Tea for Two" on the one "classical music" radio station that survives in my region. This "segregation" is presumably not based on race, or not solely on race, but rather on cultural snobbery. Moreover, Jazz became too *difficult* for the kind of ears that can be soothed by snippets of High European Kultur — or by Low Pseudo-Sexual Supermarket Rock-n-Roll, for that matter. Jazz, one fears, has become a form of mourning.

Similarly, I dare say you've never walked into an Art Museum anywhere in America and seen on the wall a framed color Sunday newspaper page of *Krazy Kat* from George Herriman's Late Period, when he attained a level of formal great-ness comparable to, say, Odilon Redon or Paul Klee. In fact, I'll bet you've never seen a single example of American cartooning in any American museum, unless you've visited a museum devoted solely to cartooning. There are a few. But heaven forbid they should be classified as ART museums! ("Pop" art consists of an ironic sneering at an absent subject; it's not *popular,* it's echt-elitist.)

Some critics might argue that comics can't be art because they're not unique items with "aura" like paintings or sculptures, but are mass-produced. Comics are non-auratic, which means *low*. The "original drawings" for comics are almost valueless because they consist simply of maquettes for printing, and are disfigured by scratch-outs and scotch-tape, and drawn on inferior acidic paper. The real comic is the printed comic, and hence there is no "art". But what about Daumier, Doré, Toulouse-Lautrec — are their prints to be considered art or non-art? The truth is simply that comics are cheap, while "real" art is very very expensive — and price has now become our sole criterion of value. Plus — laughter feels quite inappropriate in the Museum's hushed gloom. I remember at the big dada retrospective in NYC some years ago the only visitors who were laughing were a few children. Everyone else wore headphones that told them what to think and when to move on, and the silence was sepulchral. Culture itself, it seems, is a form of mourning.

It's now considered true that Herriman was African-American (from a New Orleans Creole family), although he "passed". This might well account for his outsider style: Krazy Kat is not only both male and female but also black. Under the influence of KK I first became an anarchist (as I explain in *Heresies,* my anarchist "memoirs"[1]): — not only does Kat unnaturally love Mouse (the obviously anarchistic Ignatz) but also they both continually score victories over the bastion of Law and Order, Offisa Pupp the dog (who secretly loves the Kat). The brick with which Ignatz daily beans Krazy later came to symbolize for me the mystical pain of divine love exemplified in Persian Sufi poetry. And while reading books of pop physics in the '80s such as Nick Herbert's *Quantum Reality* and *The Dancing Wu Li Masters,*[2] I came to suspect that Herriman had also unconsciously foretold or replicated the wildest theories of quantum mechanics — Schrödinger's Cat definitely appears to be an avatar of Krazy or vice

---

1 Autonomedia, Brooklyn, 2017
2 Nick Herbert, *Quantum Reality,* NY 1987; Gary Zukav, *The Dancing Wu Li Masters,* NY, 1979.

versa. I must also mention Herriman's use of language — quite delirious and at times superbly (but humorously) beautiful. I would include him among our great poets, as did e.e. cummings, in his fine preface to the first book of collected works by Herriman [*George Herriman's "Krazy Kat"*, Grosset & Dunlap, 1975]. As an artist I would rank him with our strangest brilliant visionaries such as Albert Pynkam Rider or Joseph Cornell — not because their styles are similar but because of their naïve intensity and innocent profundity. The fact that Herriman (unlike Rider or even Cornell) was hilariously funny is just the icing on the cake.

Herriman's drawing style was "slap-dash" at times. He had a daily professional task to fulfill and was not always as great as he could be. But the very quickness and looseness of his line often attains something of the spontaneous quality of zen inkbrush drawings. And in his color Sunday pages, where he was allowed to exercise control over the inks, he created a kind of art-deco Surrealist look that has never been matched in either fine or popular art. The excellent albums of reprints by Fantagraphics allow us to see almost all of his Sunday work. (His daily b&w strips are still only partly available.) And since the printed art IS the art, the act of reading these books offers a direct unmediated experience, like going to a museum to see the Picassos, only better, because you can stay home and get stoned. (Was Herriman a pot-head? One of his characters was named "Marijuana", and Krazy's "Thunderbolt tea" is highly suspect. GH spent happy time in Mexico. Newspaper readers were more innocent in those days.)

The only other American comic artist I might rank as high as Herriman would be Windsor McKay, creator (in 1907) of *Little Nemo in Slumberland*. McKay was obsessed with dreams — his earlier strip was called "Dreams of the Rarebit Fiend" — and was devoted to humorous but often terrifying nightmares worthy of Max Ernst. *Nemo's* dreamworld was less violent but deeper and more beautiful — it was printed full-page in fine colors. Unlike Herriman, McKay was an accomplished draughtsman — but his imagination was similarly unhinged. Influenced by Art Nouveau, he pre-invented the future of Surrealism, as did, say, Lewis

Carroll (also an obvious influence; Slumberland=Wonderland, Nemo=Alice). The Unconscious had only recently been "discovered" — in fact Freud's first work appeared in English two years *later* than *Little Nemo*. McKay's work seems to me highly eroticized. The sleeping boy searches every night for the Princess of Slumberland, only to be foiled by the King or his minions, including a green-faced cigar-smoking imp (son of the Goddess of the Dawn) who later becomes Nemo's best friend. Nemo dresses in gorgeous barococo costumes, as do all the denizens of Sleep, and the vertiginous perspectives of dream architecture (combination Piranesi, Escher, Versailles and Bomarzo) produce in readers the kind of sensuous swoon one associates with falling in love. Very psychedelic.

McKay is perhaps more beautiful than Herriman and less humorous, but he is capable of wonderful slapstick at times. Incidentally, he appears to have been very nearly the first creator of a commercial animated cartoon — "Gertie the Dinosaur". He travelled with the Gertie films and appeared live on stage in front of the screen, performing shtick with the lovable brontosaurus — a lost art form!

Reading McKay produces for me the same magical trance I experience with — e.g. — the *Hypnerotomachia Poliphili* or the tales of Lord Dunsany. One loses one's self there and discovers a deeper being related to the realms of Faery, beyond Time and its vicissitudes and disappointments. Is *Nemo* as great as *A Midsummer Night's Dream?* Well, maybe comparisons are invidious. But when I think of *Nemo*, I can hear the music Mendelssohn wrote for the *Dream* when he was just sixteen years old. Like the Land of Youth in Irish legend, Tír na nÓg, Slumberland can never grow old.

When I was a kid and dreamed of becoming a cartoonist, all my favorite strips already belonged to the past — *Krazy Kat*, *Little Nemo*, and Walt Kelly's *Pogo*. Kelly was my ideal. He was undoubtedly the best draughtsman in all cartooning — his handling of pen and ink and brush lavished perfection on seeming trivia such as the facial expressions of Albert the Alligator. In retrospect a lot of Kelly's liberal political satire and anti-Communism now seem a little stale; at the time I simply didn't understand it all, so it didn't bother me. At his best however Kelly was funnier than anyone, especially in the superb kinetics of the drawing and the pun-rich density of the dialogue. Like Herriman, Kelly was a genuine poet of a made-up American vernacular; and his actual poetry (composed largely by the turtle, Churchy La Femme) ranks with Edward Lear for sheer immortal Nonsense.

As with Herriman's Kokonino Kounty and McKay's Slumberland, Kelly — a true logothete — created a whole world and then dwelt in it on the imaginal level. Okeefenokee Swamp (which Kelly never visited in real life) appeared to me a kind of utopia. One summer vacation I persuaded my parents to take me there. I still think swamps are acutely poetic. As with the boat in which Alice and her sister and Lewis Carroll poled into a summer dream, Kelly's flat boats were all vehicles of real vision, moving against an exquisite background of Spanish-moss-draped trees and wading herons (who often proved talkative and ill-tempered) — moving into a wetland of Cocaigne, a Big Rock Candy marsh of . . . funny animals.

I actually disliked superheroes as a child. You could have Superman and Batman. I much preferred funny animals and kids. Since the 1950s I've read my *Pogo* book collection over and over many times — and generally I never re-read anything, feeling as I do that there are "so many books — so little time", as the t-shirt says. *Pogo* always seems new to me. And now Fantagraphics plans to publish every single strip in a series of oversize volumes (so far four have appeared) — many of which I've never ever seen. For me this is like the discovery of (say) the lost plays of Aristophanes. Well . . . better, actually.

As for funny animals, Carl Barks devoted a long career to a single dysfunctional family of ducks. Donald lives with three nephews — where are the mother and father? Donald's Uncle Scrooge with his Kaaba-full of silver dollars and greenbacks — was his sister Donald's mother? She's never mentioned. Granma Duck with her bucolic farm and her 1911 Detroit Electric flivver — is she the progenitor of the missing generation? by parthenogenesis? And why is Donald's cousin a *goose*? (— the obnoxious Gladstone Gander, whom Barks once admitted he disliked). The brilliance of this mystery lies in the surreptitious elimination of "Oedipal misery", the creation of a world in which the child's soul can live free of family. In fact Huey, Dewey, and Louie, the nephews, are the most competent and courageous of the ducks, nearly omniscient thanks to their miraculous *Junior Woodchucks' Guide.* Donald himself tries to achieve bourgeois stability but inevitably fails: he's chronically unemployed, and he never marries his long-suffering girlfriend, Daisy, which would threaten the chaste and mystical chaos in which the ducks live their lives of adventure.

The adventure is usually provided by Scrooge McDuck, who hires Donald (for derisory sums) to accompany him on perilous quests for more money. Barks meticulously researched all the exotic settings for their capers — Scotland, Alaska, Peru or whatever — and I remember thinking I was being instructed as well as entertained. I might even argue for an esoteric subtext to Barks's work — Scrooge as parodic alchemist, the Junior Woodchucks as crypto Masons.

Barks (like his Boss Walt Disney) has been lambasted as an apologist for imperialist American Capitalism, and it is true in a way. The Ducks are not anarchists like Krazy and Ignatz, or even democratic liberals like Pogo. But their antics can *also* be read as a covert satire of the values to which Donald aspires with such futile absurdity. And anyway, what kid wouldn't enjoy the primitive pleasure of diving into Scrooge's money bin? But the zillionaire's greed and guile are shown as constantly threatened (for instance by the nefarious dog burglars, the Beagle Boys) and his paranoid rage and stinginess are mocked, not idealized.

If it's possible to say that a world of silly ducks can be *beautiful*, then I would contend that Barks "The Duck Man" should be considered a great artist. Like Herriman, McKay and Kelly, he succeeded in creating a whole world — Duckburg — in which the imagination could reign: — an *alam-i mithal*, to quote the Sufi Ibn 'Arabi, or realm of archetypes.

As for funny kids, after *Little Nemo*, my favorite was *Little Lulu*. This work was drawn by various artists, nicely but not brilliantly, the real genius being the writer, John Stanley.

Lulu appeared in a 10¢ comic book, like the Ducks, and her monthly manifestations were cause for joy and satisfaction. She and her friend, Tubby, lived in the real world of suburban white America, but remained strangely free to "go out and play" on their own without adult supervision. Come to think of it, so did we. In that misty yesteryear we spent a great deal of time *outside* the family panopticon, our childhood as yet unthreatened by an antibiotic Future. Lulu has a loving family and goes to a decent school, but she remains a free spirit with a fully realized life and autonomy of her own.

Lulu constantly finds herself at odds with the neighborhood "No Girls Allowed" club. Tubby is torn between his love of Lulu and his desire to be accepted as one of the boys. Lulu is a genius, and the joke of the on-going story lies in her continual brilliant triumph over male chauvinism. She is a proto-feminist! Tubby himself is a self-proclaimed genius, a big ego with bouts of low self-esteem, but *au fond* he's as lively and imaginative as Lulu, although he tries to hide his A-plus report card from his low-brow pals in the club. As *intellectuels manqués,* I closely identified with both Lulu and Tubby. I still do.

Again, one might maintain that *Lulu* concealed an esoteric sub-text, in this case to be found not in the "real" world but in Lulu's wild imagination, the stories she tells, full of magic and witchcraft, to her rambunctious neighbor, the naughty toddler Alvin, to keep him sedated with narrative.

As some sort of polar opposite to Lulu, the Katzenjammer Kids exploded in an orgy of sadistic chaotic rage against their hapless guardian, the Captain. Based on the 19th century German children's classic, the great *Max und Moritz* (launched in 1897 by Rudolf Dirks) — the Katzenjammers were definitely anarchist, although in the end they were always spanked masochistically and mercilessly for their incredibly dangerous pranks. At some point this strip fell into copyright difficulties and spawned a number of unauthorized imitations, including *The Captain and The Kids*, and best of all, The *Kind-der-Kids*. This last masterpiece, by the famous German Expressionist artist Lyonel Feininger, who had migrated temporarily to Chicago, appeared for less than a year (1906). It proved simply too weird even for American comic aficionados. Each episode was a wildly coloristic Expressionist canvas, delirious and arcane. If this strip had survived it might well have become the greatest of all comics. But it was just too good to last.

I didn't care much for *Nancy and Sluggo* by Ernie Bushmiller, but later I came to appreciate the proto-Pop-Art draughtsmanship and cool humor that made this strip a favorite of the 1950s "New York School" of poets. However, I adulated another kid comic that had vanished before I was born but survived in paperback reprints (purchased by my father) — *Barnaby and Mr. O'Malley* by Crockett Johnson. The artist was an actual Marxist and launched his strip in *The New Masses*, but the work was scarcely overt agitprop and definitely not Socialist Realism. It concerned a little boy who acquired a fairy godfather, a pint-sized Irish pixie with pink wings in a fedora and raincoat, whose magic wand is a cheap cigar, and whose sorcery always goes comically awry. Mr. O'Malley himself is another logothete, a word-spinner, a great liar and fantasist, a blow-hard and mono-logist, who just happens to be a supernatural entity. Barnaby's world becomes saturated with magic — a talking dog (who tells long boring shaggy dog stories), a timid ghost, an invisible leprechaun with a Brooklyn accent — but his parents are convinced he's "imagining" it all, and worry about his mental health. In one classic episode they even take him to a child psychiatrist, who is of course utterly defeated by Mr. O'Malley. The few adults who actually see O'Malley think they've gone crazy — and Barnaby's parents never glimpse him. The next-door neighbor child, a practical-minded girl named Jane, sees all the supernatural creatures Barnaby hangs out with, but thinks they're silly. Although O'Malley's magic never seems to work right (if at all), somehow everything always comes out fine, with Barnaby triumphant and ever-loyal to his fairy godfather.

Johnson's drawing style was simple to the point of minimalism, with a crisp clean unadorned line that could express a great deal with a paucity of detail. But his language was lush and baroque. O'Malley was yet another great poet — of bombast and self-inflation — pure Irish *talk* in its endless flow of elegant and fractured erudition. As a kid I missed some of O'Malley's obscure allusions, but always enjoyed his cracked eloquence. Re-reading him now I realize his Joycean depth — and his crypto-revolutionary genius for cocking a snoot at the Authorities.

In a back cover blurb for the Fantagraphics re-print collection of *Barnaby* (Vol. II) Greil Marcus says:

> There's no way Jack Kerouac, along with every other self-consciously cool person in New York wasn't reading this. O'Malley turns into Neal Cassady, the guy who's not quite human, who never shuts up, who drives you crazy, and who can make anything happen, just like that.

A good guess. But the truth is (as I discovered from Neal Cassady scholar Kim Spurlock) Neal's favorite cartoon character was Major Hoople, star of *Our Boarding House* by Gene Ahearn (another Celt!). In my childhood Hoople was being drawn by other later artists but I loved him. He was an incredible fat windbag and pathological liar, a lazy parasite (on his poor wife, who ran the boarding house); the rank of major was obviously fake, and Hoople's role in life was boring the pants off the dinner guests with long tales of his wild game hunts in Africa, etc. etc. He belonged to a bachelors' secret society called The Owls, devoted to serious drinking, and wore spats and a fez. Perhaps he was another Mason, a Shriner. His favorite expression was "Egad!" — a word Cassady savored and used constantly.

Hoople gave a whole generation of future poets permission to shirk work, activate the inner Blarney stone, indulge in Eatables and Drinkables (as Horace Walpole used to say), spin yarns — and wear fezzes. The way he talked informed Neal (as did the loquacious charlatan character portrayed by W.C. Fields), and Neal helped Kerouac find his true voice — so we can say that Ahearn's Hoople is an important but forgotten influence on American Lit in the Beat and post-Beat periods. And he wasn't the only secret hipster angel of the æsthetic imagination to be born in the Comics, as we shall have further occasion to discover.

By the time I was growing up, the original *Popeye* by Segar (who died young) had been replaced by a vulgarian clone, and I failed to appreciate him. The recent reprints of Segar's work however have revealed the proletarian sailor to be a great character, malapropistic dialogist, defender of the poor and downtrodden, big-hearted and brave. True, he is not the most brilliant of intellects, and like Billy Budd, he tends to respond in awkward social situations with a punch to the snoot. But his heart is always in the right place — with the People. In fact, Popeye is a Populist. A slight shift to the left and he would have joined the Maritime Branch of the IWW.

To set off the hero's nobility, his best friend, J. Wellington Wimpy plays the archetypal mooch, liar, gourmand, work-shy bum in a derby hat and crumpled necktie. Skinny and discombobulated, Olive Oyl loves but never quite captures the eternal bachelor, Popeye, but a mysterious omnipotent baby called Swee'pea (an "orphink" as Popeye says) links their emotions.

"I yam what I yam and thass all I yam", says Popeye, echoing Nietzsche. He is the übermench hidden in the grotesquely muscled body of (yet another) unconscious poet. His adventures (involving the great villainess, the Witch of the Sea) demonstrate the dialectic of Overcoming the Uncanny. (Yes, another esoteric subtext. American comics seem to constitute a kind of volkish Vedanta.)

Parenthetically, I once saw a "Tijuana bible", one of the 8-page pornographic comic parodies printed in Mexico and still circulating around elementary school playgrounds in the '40s and '50s — this one was a take-off on Popeye, who became a veritable Priapus under the magic influence of spinach, and the art was such a perfect imitation of the original that I suspect Segar himself may have produced it. Most of the "bibles" were crudely drawn, but rumor has it that underpaid professionals sometimes took money to satirize their own (or their colleagues') *œuvres*. If the official comix served as mystic scriptures, these 8-pagers were the Kama Sutra of the American subconscious.

I've already written about Rube Goldberg in an essay on Marcel Duchamp, but I need to repeat a few points here. In 1921, while working on *The Bride Stripped Bare by Her Bachelors, Even* (a.k.a *The Great Glass*), Duchamp befriended the brilliant young American artist, Man Ray, and together they published a one-shot little magazine (in the 1980s we'd've said it was a "zine") called *New York Dada*. In it they printed an appropriated strip by popular cartoonist Rube Goldberg, whose zany and deeply critical approach to modern technology appealed to their dada sensibilities. Goldberg's hilarious machinery finds its "high" counterpart in the sexualized clockwork of *The Great Glass*, and Duchamp himself admitted (or at least hinted at) the influence. Duchamp was always cagey and closemouthed about his sources, but it's clear that he read the funny papers with pleasure. Like other French intellectuals and æsthetes he appreciated American humor in its pre-bourgeois anarchoid innocence as a pure manifestation of the unconscious. Charlie Chaplin and Buster Keaton influenced the French Surrealists and Existentialists, and I wouldn't be surprised to learn that Duchamp (like e.e. cummings) was a *Krazy Kat* fan. We know he liked *Mutt & Jeff* because he told an interviewer that the famous urinal signed "R. Mutt" was an homage to this classic strip.

Mutt & Jeff (1907) by Bud Fisher exemplifies what might be called the "homosocial" aspect of the Comix. The craft was almost exclusively male, and remains so (with a few modern exceptions such as Lynda Barry and Aline Kaminsky-Crumb). M & J began their career as race-course touts, and always retained a seedy lower-class aversion to honest work; their louche macho slapstick love/hate relation defines the strip's appeal.

Male pair-bonding proliferates in the funnies. Of course there exist highly heterosexual strips like *Li'l Abner* and *Terry and the Pirates* or *Dagwood and Blondie,* but their view of the erotic life is always weirdly skewed by residual puritanism and boyish innocence. The Tijuana bibles had to be invented to vent the pent-up psycho-sexual energies that were repressed in the newspapers and pulp comix. As we know, the artists who created such "queer" pairs as Batman and Robin or Aquaman and Aqualad, were devastated and amazed to be accused (by the Senate Investigating Committee that arose to censor the wild *imaginaire* of comic art) of homosexuality. They honestly had no idea.

An argument can be made that the child soul (or psyche if you prefer) must realize itself through ideals of comradeship and solidarity that appear (to jaundiced post-Protestant sub-therapeutic moralists) to involve highly questionable emotions. The resulting atmosphere of hyper P.C. rectitude and rigidity threatens to erase certain genuine and legitimate aspects of child-hood, and to replace them (or allow them to be replaced) with TV and videogame orgies of sick violence, consumer-fetishism, œdipal misery, and skool as capitalist brainwashing. Lost inno-cence can never be regained — which explains why the present is not a Golden Age for comic art.

Certain more-or-less anonymous and lowly old comic books exemplify this forgotten Eden of forbidden amity. *Fox & Crow* concerned two Æsopian animals living in the same hollow tree, the fox a credulous ninny, the crow a clever con-man, who were always at odds and yet somehow always reconciled. My favorites were *Heckle & Jeckle*, black magpies or crows with cod Cockney accents whose specialty was creative chaos. As a child I simply relished their shenanigans, but now I see them as esoteric avatars of the Asvin, divine twins of the *Rig Veda*, or Castor and Pollux, or Cosmos and Damian, the saints of healing. In Africa they're the Marassa, the naughty Twins who are also venerated in Haitian Voudoun. Raven is the holy Trickster in NW American Indian myth, and exemplifies the wisdom of hilarity and confu-sion. In Egypt St Anthony the Hallucinator was fed with "Raven's Bread", which might have been magic mushrooms (or ergot-ridden). In Norse legend they are Huginn and Muninn, "Thought" and "Memory", who perch on the shoulders of Odin (Hermes) and fly out to spy on the world for their one-eyed god. Unlike the raven Noah sends out after the flood they return to their patron. As *black* birds they represent the Nigredo in alchemy, the stage of darkness that must precede the Transmutation of "low" matter into the Philosopher's Stone — *hilaritas* becomes *levitas* — as Below, so Above. Secretly the Nigredo is already the gold of the Sun.

Did the creators of Heckle and Jeckle intend any of this *phantasia* of comparative mysticism? Surely not — but so what? Intention doesn't count for very much in the creation of *Art* (and alchemy is called *the* Art par excellence) — as Jarry would no doubt have conceded. What you see is what you get — but you must be prepared to *see*.

My grandmother, a lifelong Anglophile, kept her entire collection of *Punch* magazine in a closet dating back to the Early Dark Ages (when Irishmen for example were still being portrayed as comical apes). When I came to visit her I'd spend many happy afternoons on the floor leafing through issue after issue looking for my favorite cartoonists. The ones I remember best are Rowland Emmett, who specialized in trains and trams (like the British equivalents of our "Toonerville Trolley") and is now sadly forgotten; and Ronald Searle, a great pen-man, still remembered for such masterpieces as *The Bells of St Trinian's* (about a boarding school for evil little girls). The class and race prejudices sailed over my head at the time. I had to live in England for several years later in life to understand that *all* British humor is based on Class War — including such supposedly "whacky" examples as Monty Python or the "Carry On" film series. The proles are slagging off the bourgeoisie, the middleclass is sneering at the workmen and idle aristo's, and the upper class is guffawing at everyone except themselves. Very weird. But then they think the same of us. So much for a common language and shared heritage.

The French and Belgians have made great contributions to the art. *Tintin* may be reactionary but it's also highly entertaining and beautifully drawn, and the hardback album format is quite satisfying. *Asterix* appeals to my Celtic chauvinism, and is also nicely researched and well done. And I'd like to mention a French title unknown in the US, *The Masked Cucumber (Le concombre masqué)*. Really odd.

By the time my generation reached high school, the Senate hearings had led to voluntary self-censorship of the art under the Comic Decency Code, and everything had become far duller and more conformist. Mickey Mouse, once a wild adventurer, now wore slacks and golf shoes and lived in a suburb of the Californian Dream. The hideous horror series EC Comics disappeared (it gave me nightmares and even now I confess I dislike it), and some of the censored artists like Will Elder and Jack Davis decided to take revenge by founding a magazine called *Mad*, devoted to pushing the envelope of bad taste to the limit. The first twenty-five issues, edited by Harvey Kurtzman, were really great. Our parents didn't "get it", which definitely increased the allure.

By the '60s those who had grown up on comic books and then gone on to read *Mad* were ready for the underground comix of the Psychedelic era, such as those published by Zap. One world-class genius emerged from this milieu — R. Crumb, the American Daumier. He took the innocent brilliance of the tradition and transmuted it into genuine Swiftian satire, without losing the exuberance and sheer hilarity of his models, even in his bitterest and most pornographic moments. And he still draws like an angel. Aside from his work the '60s produced a few other masterpieces, such as Gilbert Sheldon's "Fabulous Furry Freak Brothers", devoted to extended narratives of pot-head farce, and the Celine-like dark visions of S. Clay Wilson.

As for contemporary cartooning — including the tiresome superhero crap still being served up by Marvel — I find little to admire. The newspaper comic page is devoid of interest (except maybe *Doonesbury*). Hardly anyone seems bothered to learn how to draw, and the supposed humor of the alt.comics strikes me as snarky post-modern pseudo-irony mixed with sheer negativity and depression. However there are a few shining exceptions, among whom I might mention Matt Groening, creator of *The Simpsons* and the even better but neglected *Life in Hell*. But my favorite has to be Ben Katchor, who first came to my attention in the *NY Press* with an on-going epic called *Julius Knipl, Real Estate Photographer*. Using a gray wash technique that references faded b&w photographs, he follows his hero around a lost New York of neglected old buildings, pathetic small businesses, urban melancholy, forgotten back streets in the other boroughs, sad scenes of human futility — and he captures an America known to no other artists since George Bellows and the Ashcan School — but with a gentle sense of humor and sympathy for the existential human condition. He's proved to be no flash in the pan, but like Crumb he keeps on producing one terrific series after another. His latest — *Hand Drying in America*, devoted to useless machines and the idiots who manufacture and use them, strikes me as one of his best.

For an honorable mention I recommend Peter Blegrad's *Leviathan*. Generally I don't go for this sort of thing — angst and dark forebodings mingled with menace — but Blegrad manages to make it funny and even profound. And mystical.

This is not an essay on comedy in general but something has to be said about the mutual influence of movies and comics. Before the censorship imposed by "Comic Decency" and the Hollywood "Code", film and funnies both embodied a special American apolitical anarchy that has no parallel in any other culture. As mentioned, European intellectuals admired this feral brilliance and sometimes aspired to re-create it — or transmute it into serious art as with dada and Surrealism.

This extreme humor was based in part on violence, misogyny, racism, repressed sexual perversion and other Bad Things that eventually came to upset the sensibilities of the "emerging" middle class and its hegemons. Just to take one example, the silent two-reelers made by Fatty Arbuckle and Buster Keaton now seem both transgressive and utterly transcendent, maybe the funniest films ever made, but completely heartless. I suspect that Fatty was unfairly framed in the notorious *Lustmord* case that put an end to his career, at least partly because his humor had gone beyond the bounds of what Freud called "Civilization" and its restraining Order. If Buster escaped perhaps this was due to his different style — so pokerfaced and impenetrable — more sly than Fatty, but equally mad. The archetypal Keaton moment for me is the scene where he innocently acquires an anarchist's black bomb and lights his cigarette from its fizzing fuse — then tosses it idly over his shoulder, where it blows up a horde of police who happen (for some reason) to be following him. The "Keystone Kops" image of societal oppression as ludicrous farce, constantly deflated and even destroyed by free-spirited clowns, lies at the root of the perhaps not-so-unconscious anarchism of early film comedy in America.

We've already noted the influence of W.C. Fields on a series of cartoon humbugs and monologists — and perhaps the influence went both ways. The physically "impossible" stunts of film comics such as Harold Lloyd may have derived from a desire to replicate the fantasy-world pratfalls and disasters of the funny papers. And vice-versa. But the area where a relation between comics and film becomes transparent is of course the animated cartoons.

There's always existed an overlap between newspaper cartooning and animation. As noted, Windsor McKay pioneered the animated cartoon; Walt Kelly once worked for Walt Disney. Mickey Mouse began his career in animation and only later branched out into print genres. An attempt was made to animate *Krazy Kat*, but it failed (nevertheless it influenced the successful *Felix the Cat* films).

Obviously I could write another whole essay on animation, but I just wanted to glance at it in the context of cartooning in general as a "lively art" worthy of æsthetic analysis and critical canonization. In my childhood we enjoyed animation in color at the movie theater (along with newsreel, short and double feature) and at home on b&w TV every Saturday morning. Who remembers Farmer Gray and his cows, drunk on XXX applejack and dancing to dixieland jazz? (In fact this was the first jazz we suburban white kids ever heard.)

The great producers were the Fleischer Brothers, Warner Brothers, and Walt Disney. In some ways the Fleischers appear supreme if only because "first thought is best thought" and they came first — but also because they were so vulgar and transgressive. I'll mention only one of their masterpieces, "St James Infirmary" with Betty Boop and music by the great Cab Calloway, a veritable hoodoo spell, a mini-opera of dark enchantment. It is true that the Boop artists drew her, one frame out of every dozen or so, without her flapper's short skirt, naked from waist to shoes; but that one frame was seen only at a subliminal level (I learned this from the official Boop cartoonist of the 1980s, who was my neighbor on the Lower East Side). No wonder the Puritans associated cartoons with the "dark tide of mud", as Freud said, the eruption of the occult forbidden unconscious into daylight.

Warner Brothers created some of the deathless masterpieces of the genre. Daffy Duck, Elmer Fudd, The Roadrunner all deserve adulation, but the real star of Warners was Bugs Bunny. I've said this before, but it bears repeating, that Bugs has deep roots. We can trace him back to the African folktales of The Trickster Rabbit, whom most of us know through the Uncle Remus tales of Joel Chandler Harris. Br'er Rabbit in turn can be identified with a real person, the great rakehell bi-sexual Arab poet Abu Nuwas, who appears as a character in *The 1001 Nights*. In Africa, where these stories were wildly popular, Abu Nuwas's exploits were blended in with those of the traditional trickster Rabbit. This ancestry explains Bugs's sexual fluidity, his appearances in drag, his kissing the hapless Elmer Fudd and making him blush pink. It explains why Bugs is considered amongst African-Americans to be a Black hero. And it also explains why Bugs was adopted as mascot of the Chicago Surrealists, my admired and respected colleagues.

Walt Disney, the Confucian sage as Ezra Pound called him, belongs on the Right of the world of cartooning, but there's no denying his greatness. I once met one of his artists, who told me that Walt told them to take as long as they needed to do the best work possible on the full-length cartoon features. Disney spent so much money on these works that it took twenty years for some of them to turn a profit. He built Disneyland and churned out family entertainment flicks primarily in order to finance the cartoons. He coddled the artists and paid them well. In short he really was a visionary and *auteur*. The cartoons are made with the most complex technology ever achieved (at least before computers, which have spoiled animation with their soulless perfection). "Full animation", Disney style, as opposed to "stop-animation" (e.g.

The Flintstones) uses the same ratio of frames to action as photographic film, and deploys four distinct levels of kinetic imagery. There has never been a technically more perfect cartoon than *Fantasia*. We may regret that its hero is Mickey Mouse, but the creative chaos that's often lacking in Walt's other work here emerges into full view. Disney transcends himself.

We've entertained the notion that comics possess an esoteric "sub-text" as it were, but on what basis could such an assertion be defended? I would refer the reader to the phenomenon of the 16th and 17th century Emblem Books for an explanation. When the Renaissance sages re-discovered Late Antique Egypt and saw hieroglyphics for the first time, they assumed that each glyph directly presented a word, and that the system was imbued with magic. To be able to write hieroglyphics promised a kind of occult power that mere alphabetic literacy seemed to lack. Misled by such texts as Horapollo's *Hieroglyphica*[3], a 5th century A.D. text based on interesting but faulty information, and rediscovered in the 15th century, the Renaissance mages devoted huge efforts to "cracking" hieroglyphics; but lacking a Rosetta Stone (and the knowledge that some glyphs represent sounds rather than things), they failed. So they decided to invent their own hieroglyphs by breaking down the *image-as-word* into image AND word. (See Iversen's *Egyptian Hieroglyphs* for the full fascinating story.[4])

The Image, as Giordano Bruno noted, can be deployed, via Imagination, as a form of magic that will "enchain" those who see it — and combined with text this magic (unconscious) influence can be developed or given content, so the two levels reinforce each other with a kind of mirroring or multiple feedback effect that can be theorized as "occult" in the sense of *hidden* or psyche-logical rather than overt and merely discursive. The result of this process was the Emblem, the symbolic picture plus caption.

---

3 See Peter Lamborn Wilson, "Speaking in Hieroglyphics", in *Alexandria 3*, Phanes Press, Grand Rapids, MI, 1995, pg. 307.
4 Erik Iversen, *The Myth of Egypt and Its Hieroglyphs in European Tradition*, Princeton, 1993.

Emblems could be merely allegorical, but when used to convey esoteric information such as alchemy they could become imbued with a power that later held great appeal for Jungian analysts — not to mention (as Ioan Couliano pointed out) advertisers, spin-doctors, propagandists, and educators. "Image Magic" *works*. It plunges us into the Subconscious and then textually directs the resultant released potency toward some end — whether psychic illumination or soul-slavery. This explains how modern Pop artists appropriated the comics (under the banner of Irony) to create powerful artworks that sell for millions.

When I use the term "Surrealism" in connection with the Comix, I'm not thinking so much of the early Marxist-Freudian period of that movement. Later, after their disillusionment with such orthodoxies, the Surrealists achieved a much more resonant synthesis (or so I feel) based on — e.g. — the mad utopian visionary Charles Fourier, Hermeticism and alchemy, and a politics tending away from authoritarianism and toward anarcho-syndicalism and anarchism. Of course the Comix were largely unconscious of any such proclivities. Rube Goldberg expressed amused annoyance at being dragooned into dada, and never ceased to make fun of "serious art". The Surrealists however were devoted precisely to the making-conscious of the unconscious, the overt return of the repressed, the deliberate revolution of the Imagination. Their tragedy was to succeed all too well. Not only did their art enter the ArtWorld and become hideously expensive, but their discoveries were ripped off by advertisers and brainwashers and turned against the revolt of the unconscious toward its commodification and militarization.

And today humor itself has lost its innocence and become "knowing", more Post-modern irony than childlike eruption of divine chaos. Comix are now more generally concerned with sneering than with laughing. "Pop Surrealism" becomes self-parody rather than revolutionary æsthetic.

To give them their due, the remnants of the Surrealist Movement have resisted this trend and continue to insist on their insurrectionary loyalties. One might wish they could discover a new style to replace the old one that should have passed away with Breton, or at least with the great Leonora Carrington (who lived to nearly a hundred and died only a few years ago). Still, it's cheering to note that traditional Surrealism appears to be quite out of style just now. Not that one can buy Ernst or Dali at bargain prices, but the pundits of ArtWorld seem far more engaged with neo-abstract expressionism (and PoMo Irony) than with the strange and overly-sincere beauty — or humor — of Surrealism. The Un- or Sub- conscious has gone out of fashion and been replaced by pills and the Internet. And the Comix, as I pointed out earlier, have never been admitted to the temple of Real Art anyway.

This disdain, this dismissal of Comix as merely popular and ergo unimportant, paradoxically may help to save them from the kind of commodification that has ruined so many pristine phenomena in our culture. We should perhaps actually pray that the Art Moghuls never discover what *native genius* they've missed or dissed. The fact that there seems no way of selling an old yellowing Sunday newspaper comic page for thirty million dollars may prove to be the art's salvation, or at least its preservation. Thanks to the recent reprints of *Fantagraphics* and other smaller publishers, it may still happen that the masterpieces discussed here could fall into the hands of children still capable of innocent delight and rebellious fantasy.

If this were to happen we could pray that Surrealism itself would not die but change and find new ways to confront the Totalitarianism of the Image and the enchainment of the Imagination. Or is that hoping for too much?

Why I Hate the Bourgeoisie

Let me start by saying that I'm going to speak only about America. Elsewhere in the world there may still exist real peasants and workers, real leftists, socialists, syndicalists, agrarian radicals in the old-fashioned senses of those terms (maybe even aristocrats!). Peru? Greece? I don't know. It would be nice to imagine.

Here, according to consensus opinion, there can no longer be found a working class in the traditional meaning of the word. We are all middleclass now, or so we say. The former working class is now said to be transformed: obese, reactionary, Republican, would-be petty bourgeois, utterly committed to loyal support for the One Percent and its billionaires, happy to work at shit jobs for minimum wages, patriotic, racist, xenophobic, etc. etc. (Recently they've shown vague signs of "waking up" into a more active *ressentiment* and crypto-fascist "populism".) Our remnant "poor" are supposed to consist only of "racial minorities"— Blacks and Native Americans, for instance, who are seen as outside the class system — beneath it. Everyone else is said to be middleclass, even the Wealthians, who (according to a recent survey) actually work more hours than anyone else. The One Percent — the CEO class — are simply the biggest wage slaves of all — not idle dukes and earls. *Are* there still any idle rich? So — the middle class is split between two branches, as it were — the red state types and the blue state types. The obese Republicans and the slender Democrats. They despise each other with true class hatred. They threaten civil war. But *au fond* they're just — the bourgeoisie. You could perhaps think of them as the Former Lower class and the Former Upper Class. The Former Lowers espouse the class values of the Uppers (because some day thanks to hard work and virtue they hope to be RICH) — while the Former Uppers pretend to adhere to working class virtues — they're "pro-labor" and "anti-racist" and upset by inequality and the environmental crisis — but they nevertheless remain pure bourgeoisie. They're not union members (who *is*?), they don't socialize with Blacks and Indians, they spend their big wages on big houses and big cars and eat up huge amounts of energy and "resources" and give nothing back. They waste fortunes on "health food" and diet supplements and solar power and electric cars. And they *hate* the "lower classes" (those awful bigots! Those racists! So not hip and sophisticated! So *Republican!*) As the Situationists realized — it's all pure Spectacle.

Somewhere — almost invisible — a few farmers may linger on, a few poor country folk who work seasonally, hunt, grow a garden, smoke a bit of weed, drink some beer. Somewhere maybe a few unionized factory workers are singing old IWW songs. And do there still "survive" a handful of actual bohemians, refuseniks, garret-dwellers, kultur-martyrs, unable to sell out to the Hipster Art World Market because they're too fucking weird — genuine Outsiders? Maybe. I hope so.

But everyone else is — *bourgeois*.

Now as Nietzsche said somewhere, one cannot understand disease unless one has been sick. Hopefully one *recovers* — this is the essential Nietzschean position: to have been sick and to have *gotten better*. This and only this constitutes true strength or self-power. Otherwise there can only be — *ressentiment*, bad conscience, masked slavishness. I was born middleclass. Let me not dissemble. There were "white trash" connections in my family, there were "aristocratic" pretensions in some branches. But both my parents were college-educated wage slaves — professional educators. Democrats. Liberals. If I failed to make the grade, if I dropped out of my "ivy league" university, if I refused to work, if I devoted my life to art, if I never made any money but lived off unearned income (basically my father's savings) so as to be "independently poor", if I identified as a bohemian, an outsider, an anarchist — it was all in an attempt to *escape being bourgeois*. Did I succeed? I can't say for sure. All I know is: I hate the bourgeoisie. Maybe that makes me "self-hating", like that famous mythical beast, the self-hating Jew. I'd rather claim to be a true bohemian, a lumpen-prole criminal poet. But someone else will have to judge. And since almost all my friends are — in fact — middle class, who will judge justly?

**

The worst thing I can think to say about this America is that it has corrupted the authentic. Almost everything has become a representation of itself, a simulacrum of the once-real. Everything presents itself with an ironic smirk. In the cool new Brooklyn, for instance, some old store called, let's say "Acme Shoes", will be transformed into a kultur bar and keep the old sign and the name — ACME SHOES. The old church is now an arts center. Old photographs of coal miners with blacklung disease hang over your table in the upscale "veggie" burger and latté café — touch of gritty realismo. In the lobby of the new yuppie apartment building on E. 7th street you can see artsy b&w photos of the old Dominican gardeners and drug-raddled punk squatters who were evicted so the building could be built. That thinly-bearded hipster in "narrow clothes" is (ironically) a hedge fund manager.

An important part of the hip-bourgeois self-presentation lies in our belief (albeit a somewhat ironic belief) in our sexual liberation. The Sexual Revolution is over and We won. Don't we have gay marriage now? And abortion? Internet porn? The truth however appears to be that we have displaced libido into the phony "representation of the once-real" that passes for our "obscure object of desire". Actually many Americans secretly hate sex. They find "relationships" sticky and reproduction awkward and expensive. If it weren't for immigration the U.S. rate of population increase (especially of middleclass whites) would be declining. In places where *everyone* is middleclass and white it *is* declining. Well — more room for trees, you say. Or anyway — more room for parking lots.

The subconscious repression of desire manifests as the ubiquity of the *Image of Desire*, according to the Law that as something vanishes it becomes the subject of universal "discourse". Advertising constitutes our richest source of true desire, but the commodity itself becomes less and less *embodied*. The new desideratum is some little grey machine that "represents" the now-vanished social network. They say people under twenty can't even look each other in the eyes. Education consists of massive on-line alienation. Relation"ships" are carried out by tweet as if we were all "boys in bubbles", lost astronauts in some PK Dick story or essay by Jean Baudrillard — "in touch" like gnostic ghosts — in pure spirit — not in the flesh. "Community" means our Facebook "friends". We have achieved lift-off.

The repression of desire manifests most clearly in the bourgeois "care of the self". Children cannot be allowed to experience one moment of aimless unsupervised play or empty time. Every hour of the day must be enriched. Boredom must be banished with pills or therapy. Soon we'll all grow up and die with robot nannies and cyber care providers — in fact we already do: we have the Internet. Video games. TV Screenal abjection from infancy till senility. The electronic hearth is our cozy, all-consuming holocaust. We're all burnt sacrifices to the Bourgeois self, our anodyne substitute for Moloch. We're obsessed with *health* because we can't admit we're *sick* — sick to death of Civilization. And health is a commodity, just like all the others.

The result of this therapy of the enhanced bourgeois Self is a thoroughly self-conscious Hamlet-type, unable to act because too self-aware to engage in any primitive will to power. And yet this self-awareness turns out to be a disguised form of false consciousness, a profound *lack of presence* to one's self, a crippled beingness. Compared to this *mauvaise conscience* can we imagine a more "primitive" and more authentic self, spontaneous, acting directly on desire and yet desiring a true *communitas* with others — a self both free and non-alienated? A self without "character armor" — a non-bourgeois self? Where shall we find it? And now that it's been lost, can it ever be *recovered*?

In a world of commodification and representation of the self, it seems to me that the one thing remaining that should smack of authentic immediacy is the *artwork* with its "aura", its unique encapsulation of an otherwise lost creativity and presence to itself. Even post-Duchampian, post-Warholian irony-art might still be authentic æsthetic one-of-a-kind ART, and thus perhaps the only guaranteed solid commodity in a universe of ætherial rip-offs and reproductions; thus the obscene inflation of the art market since (approximately) the 1970s. Art is no longer "revolutionary" as with Surrealism or Fluxus. It's not meant to "change the world" (as Marx demanded of philosophy) — or even to "change your life", as Rilke's angel suggested. There no longer persists any avantgarde belief that "everyone must be an artist" as Beuys put it. All that died with the gold standard and Latin in high school. 1968 came and went, LSD came and went, and everything collapsed into *pure money. Infinite debt.* No more bohemia. The last possible Outside is — mere failure. Let us embrace it.

"Democratic" America is not supposed to have "class warfare" (that's *England,* not US). We may have race war, but not class hatred. But that's a myth — pure bullshit. For a start, race hatred is actually a form of class hate — and it manifests amongst Smug Liberals in two modes: avoidance of actual contact with non-White people (while maintaining that one supports anti-racist politics) — and hatred of White people who do not listen to NPR and read the *New York Times* and eat health food and send their spawn to good colleges and drive hybrid cars and have solar panels on their garage rooves. Middlebrow hate and disdain for lowbrows — social-Darwinian racism or classism — what's the difference?

Thanks to the universal middleclass we are all data processors now. No more Jeffersonian yeoman farmers. No more proletarian wealth-producers. ("Wealth-producers" now means internet app start-up technocrat entrepreneurs and "disruptors"). Work on screens, play on screens — die on screens. (How we adore our cherished representations of ultra-violence — death porn is our last real kick.) "The cruel instrumentality of reason"? — hey, that's our *livelihood* you're talking about!

We live in a world of bad taste and *bad design* so universal we've forgotten what good design might be. And why? Because Kapitalism would perish without planned obsolescence and shoddy crap that makes you want to go out and buy more crap in the hope (i.e. faith) that Progress will make better . . . crap. Oh, we've already "survived" the famous crisis of overproduction — long ago. We out-produced Communism in 1989 and drove it into extinction. The Cold War is over and *we won*! And this is your "peace dividend" — a cheap computer. And another cheap computer and another. Bourgeois Pig Heaven.

Is there anything *real* left in America? Whenever I see something really *sad* and *poor* — something that's still itself and not an ironic take on what it used to be — something authentic — weak — almost invisible — something with *wabi* as the Zen æstheticians say — I burst into tears. Well — metaphorically anyway if not actually. But sometimes — yes, actual tears. An old barn. An empty fallow field. A discarded wooden tray. A peeling hand-painted sign for an abandoned motel. A raggedy weed growing through the broken concrete of a loading dock behind a failed big-box store out on the lonesome highway to nowhere.

Nature is vanishing — maybe Nature has already gone, and been replaced by the Nature Channel. A cellphone tower on every mountain. Anthropocene die-out. Fukushima sushi. The arctic as one big melted methane fart. The measure of Nature's death is the triumph of the bourgeoisie. When the last idle artist gets a credit card and the last hunter/gatherer dies of mercury poisoning, the middleclass will reign alone and unchallenged — over an ersatz world.

Satanic Mills

I

And did these feet in ancient times
Walk upon Englands mountains green:
And was the holy Lamb of God,
On Englands pleasant pastures seen?

And did the Countenance Divine,
Shine forth upon our clouded hills?
And was Jerusalem builded here,
Among these dark Satanic Mills?

Bring me my Bow of burning gold:
Bring me my Arrows of desire:
Bring me my Spear: O clouds unfold!
Bring me my Chariot of fire!

I will not cease from Mental Fight,
Nor shall my sword sleep in my hand:
Till we have built Jerusalem,
In Englands green & pleasant land.

—William Blake, *Milton*, Preface

Blake's vision — genuine prophetic vision — of the Industrial Revolution is encapsulated in that one phrase, "dark Satanic Mills", which always conjures for me a childhood memory of the New Jersey Turnpike somewhere around Secaucus, flat swamps lined with dozens of tall petroleum cracking towers, huge H.G. Wellsian alien structures belching infernal flames into a vast polluted night. In those dear dead days New Jersey was the most toxic state in the Union, an honor that now belongs to Louisiana. (New Jersey is merely number six.) The cracking towers have long since disappeared, stalked off to Mexico I imagine, leaving the Turnpike a mere ghost of its former evil but massively impressive self. Even most of the "industrial waste" of American post-1950s ironic/romantic landscape has been cleared away and tidied up, almost turned into viable real estate. We live in the Information Economy now, and information is nothing if not *clean*.

Another biblical-level jeremiad-evocation of the Industrial Revolution flowed from the pen of F. Engels, who was himself by profession part of the Problem as much as he yearned to be part of the Solution. He knew the Ugly Spirit of Productive Capitalism from within, and conjured its horrors like a scientific Dickens. Without his intimate embedding in the dark heart of Progress, Marx's bookish soul could never have achieved its apotheosis. And yet somehow they both failed to see that the *Factory itself* was evil, at a deeper level even than the appropriation of labor value by Capital. The young Marx of the unpublished *Philosophical Notebooks* of 1844 seemed almost to understand and express this evil in his analysis of "alienation", but later he lost the insight in his fervor for the dictatorship of the proletariat.

The people who really grasped this fact — the sheer wickedness of technology — were, of course, the people. The victims of the Industrial Revolution were the workers, and the real rebels against it were not the intellectuals or the economists but the Luddites. Since they were uneducated and inarticulate, they expressed their critique of technology not with printing presses but with sledgehammers. As Kirkpatrick Sale put it, their "rebellion against the Future" was later ignored or disparaged by Marxist historians because it was anti-progress, anti-scientific-technological-rational ideological Enlightenment. The only intellectuals who really understood Luddism were the Romantic poets, Shelley and Byron especially, and even before them Blake. But according to the Marxologists, Romanticism itself constitutes a form of Reaction — and Shelley after all was an anarchist! The Marxist historians so besmirched (and then buried) the memory of the real Luddites that today the term has come to mean simple -minded ignorant backward technophobes, blind to the glories of (say) the iPhone, the kind of futile cranks who dislike the Holy Automobile or the Neutron Bomb or vaccination.

Of course the Luddites never opposed *techné* itself — they themselves were largely loom-workers and stockingers. What they hated was the *mechanized* loom which threatened to "automate their jobs" and put them out of work, or at least force them out of their homes (where they worked) and into the soulless factories. It's fascinating to me that the mechanized loom is now recognized as the "ancestor" of the computer. If any machine today represents the "Satanic" principle, it's the computer. The Industrial Revolution is over, and "we" won. Filthy exploitative factories have been evolved out of existence, or anyway out of sight. Nanotechnology will solve all the remaining "problems" of the contemporary world: — air pollution, drunk driving, birth defects, low I.Q.'s, melting glaciers, and the totalitarian unending war economy. The world will become green green green, capitalism will be clean, and America once again lean and mean — the Sole Hegemon. And the stock market will just go on rising unto eternity, and all manner of things will be well. And if you believe that, I have a nice bridge in Brooklyn you might want to buy.

Progress comprises not only the historical error of predatory capitalism, it was also the historical error of the Left. "Everyone" fell for the myth of Progress except for a few disgruntled ultra-conservatives and mystical monarchists — and a few luddite/proto-hippy leftists and spiritual anarchists. To this day if you read liberal middlebrow publications like *The New York Review of Books,* you will find, if the question of Progress arises, that anyone who opposes it must by definition be a dark Reactionary. The notion of revolutionary anti-tech Romanticism simply does not exist for these pundits. They cannot even imagine a rebel against the new Social Darwinism who is not a braindead Creationist Christian bigot. Progress has its crisis mode, of course; something must be done to stop global warming before it's too late; perhaps the One Percent should be gently persuaded to give up a few trillion to help prop up Big Government. But basically, fear not, Science will find a way. Computers will make everyone smarter, and soon no one will ever vote Republican again.

Or so the deluded yuppie bourgeois soi-disant Masters of Reality devoutly believe. Meanwhile the *real* Masters of the Universe are slaves to Pure Money, and Money is "free" to multiply itself unto infinity, and the 6000 CEOs are richly rewarded for their obsequious lickspittle loyalty to Money, and *nothing is going to get "better".*

"Progress" means bigger parking lots and shopping malls, more gadgets you simply can't survive without buying, new gadgets next year that make the old gadgets look like horseless carriages, medicine to keep you older and sicker longer and longer so you'll buy more medicine — and more endless war to stimulate an economy that would otherwise collapse under the burden of universal Debt — the Ponzi Scheme of Speculative High Speed Flash Usury Investment in Death Futures. Capitalism will profit even from the End of the World — in fact it is already doing so. This IS the Future, sucker — hope you like it so far.

Progress is Reaction. Civilization IS its discontents.

**

In the late 18th century a group of brilliant middleclass political radicals and scientists in England founded a sort of informal anti-Royal Society to pursue their own agenda, and called it the *Lunar Society* (because they met once a month, but also because their intentions were perhaps a bit shady). Josiah Wedgewood, the great ceramicist and ardent Abolitionist; James Watt, inventor of the steam engine; Joseph Priestley, radical nonconformist theologian and inventor of many things (including seltzer water!); and Erasmus Darwin, grandfather of Charles and pioneer Linnaean botanist; these geniuses comprised the core Lunar membership. The French Revolution in its early beneficent period (before the Regicide, the Terror and Napoleon) galvanized these men as it did the Romantic poets including Blake (friend of Thomas Paine), Wordsworth, Coleridge, etc. As a result, the "King and Church" reactionaries were outraged and declared war on these would-be revolutionary "leftists". A

mob burned down Priestley's house and laboratory, and he ended
by fleeing to America in 1794, and settling in Pennsylvania.
Coleridge and Southey planned to do the same; they were all
going to start an intentional community, the *Pantisocracy*, based
on egalitarian principles. But only Priestley and his family ever
made the move. The others stayed in England. Some of them
shifted to the Right as the French debacle descended into World
War. A few such as Erasmus Darwin remained loyal to their
principles.

Darwin wrote one of the most delightful long poems in
English literature, *The Botanic Garden*, an epic about the sexual
life of plants, based on Linnaeus, and couched in symbolism
derived from Darwin's deep affection for old-fashioned Hermeticism. The Romantics in general took a passionate interest in
occultism and alchemy, pagan neoplatonism and the like. Priestley's fascination with gases, for instance[1], owed a great deal
to alchemist Francis von Helmont, who coined the word
"gas" (from *chaos*). We'll return later to the role of Hermeticism
in the emergence of modern science.

**

The tragedy of the Lunar Society consists of the brilliance
of its members being subverted by History into the opposite of
what they intended. Their idea of Progress, naïve and sentimental
perhaps, was nevertheless heart-felt and positive: they wanted
peace and plenty for all, freedom and equality, and the reign of
creative Imagination. Instead, they gave birth to the Industrial
Revolution. The Royal Society devoted itself to coming up with
great ideas to nurture British Empire and British Trade — the
Lunar Society cherished a very different dream — but in the end
both groups contributed to the emergence of Capitalism and

---

[1] which was shared by Coleridge's friend Sir Humphrey Davy, inventor of ni-
trous oxide — the poets all sampled this, the first "psychedelic drug".

colonialist imperialism. Inventors always fancy their inventions will bring peace to the world — even Alfred Nobel believed this. — but in fact all technology tends towards oppression and immiseration. It may increase wealth (for a few at least) but it cannot free the human spirit because in essence it consists of the *opposite* of the free spirit.

Thus for instance in Scotland the whole idea of *Improvement,* especially in the rationalization of agriculture, was made to feed into the post-1745 Clearances of the Jacobite Highlands, turning half the country into unpopulated sheep farms and hunting preserves for English aristocrats (the Scottish Whig aristo's were equally guilty). This explains why the Scottish Romantics, like Robert Burns, were both Jacobites *and* leftist radicals. In England meanwhile a similar ideology of Improvement led to yet more Enclosures; the denial of common right in land to the rural poor, who as a result were transmogrified into the proletariat — including the Luddites — and made to work in factories, move into polluted cities, while the rich and titled landlords consolidated their country demesnes. The excess population could be turned into colonists and soldiers and used to oppress the "natives" of India and China, etc. All the efficiency and technical brilliance led directly to the Satanic Mills — to the Industrial Revolution — and eventually to the marvelous postmodern utopia we call Now — to the rule of wealthian Vampires over wage-slave zombies in the gemütlich grand-guignol of Too-Late Cognitive Kapitalismo — the Anthropocene Extinction.

In this scenario I have to blame even some of my gurus in the anarchist movement of the 19th century such as Prince Peter Kropotkin, who praised the factories of the Future, when the workers would become their own bosses. Kropotkin must be cherished for his critique of Darwinian or Social Darwinian Evolution (in Part One of *Mutual Aid*) — a question we must return to — but as a "workerist" (not to mention his capitulation to the militarists in WW I) he must be severely criticized. The Factory *in itself* is the site of alienation. What must be overcome is "Work" *per se* — whether the factory be seen as industrial or post-industrial, as old-time sweatshop or computer-driven precarious shit-work office of the PoMo "new class" and its epigones. Forget labor unions — they're dead. Forget the Keynesian utopia of Leisure for All — it's stillborn. The real reality is Work — Consume — Die. The only real 19th century critics of this model were the Romantics and the Individualist Anarchists inspired by Stirner and Nietzsche. Nowadays their heirs are the Green Anarchists and neo-nihilists, the Anti-Civilization Primitivists and the Mexican terrorists who are assassinating nanotechnologists.

And you've probably never even heard of these people — unless you're already one of us.

II

The other day I heard of an old Armenian guy in Brooklyn who's still producing beach umbrellas (although he's rented his upstairs loft to an artists' collective). He's probably a rapacious sweatshop boss, but he's also probably the last umbrella maker in America. Proper Americans no longer soil themselves in the lowly sarkic fallen realm of mere material production. Umbrellas are made by Taiwanese coolies. Farming is done by agro-industrial GM robots (or by a few neo-hippy CSA organic niche market idealists and struggling permaculturists). The total agricultural work-force in the US today is below .01%. NY State in 1900 was 40% forested, but is now 90% overgrown with useless woodlots and abandoned farms. The big California combines actually ship their produce to Mexico for packaging — and the crops are grown by illegal Mexican immigrants. The small farm has become a hobby for the rich. Agrarian radicalism died because the agrarian economy died. And so on. You've heard it already a hundred times. Entrepreneurial democracy died because small businesses were crushed by Walmart and Amazon. The working-class left and the unions died because factories moved to Hell — and money went to Heaven.

Capitalism declared the End of History (i.e., the end of the Historical Movement of the Social, the *dialectic*) in 1989. The Market was now *free*, meaning that money is free to do what it wants to do, and you're free to choose product A or product B. But you're not free not to choose. Imagine trying to hold down a job in America without owning a car, a computer and a cell phone. You need to buy; resistance is futile. You need to go into debt because your job (if you have one) doesn't pay enough to live on. Capitalism as Ponzi Scheme demands that markets expand. Ergo you must borrow and buy — q.e.d. Only the rich can afford not to consume, to be thin. The American poor are obese.

Where I live the economy looks like this: people who used to farm end up paying huge taxes on land that produces no income, so they sell off to developers and move to a doublewide in Florida. People who used to work in cigar factories and ladies' garment ateliers in the County capital are now chronically unemployed, because all production has vanished. If they're lucky they can be Greeters at Walmart. Young people can go to college if they agree to go into debt for life — otherwise they can flip burgers or get into heroin. The only really viable business is selling off our green and pleasant land as real estate to refugees from the Big City. "Environmental activism" around here means protecting the *viewshed* from ghastly blots like cement mines or publicly-owned land. Not in my backyard. Move to Mexico. I want my McMansion, my SUV, my green clean conscience, my locavore gourmet food, my yoga lessons, and fuck you and your *needs* (much less *your* desires).

Not that I don't sympathize with the green middleclass exurbanite artists and retired stockbrokers — heck, some of them are my friends. One of them might even be *me*. But I'm not kidding myself that fleeing to "paradise" makes me an angel of light.

**

The Post-Fordist Information Economy itself is trumped by an even higher form of Predatory Capitalism — speculative investment — or as it used to be called, USURA. Financial capital can gobble up productive capital like so many hamburgers and shit it out as pure profit. Why *make* anything out of matter when you can make money out of *nothing*? Bankers create money by lending ten times their actual assets — if they're honest. If they're really hip they'll lend a hundred times or more — who can stop them? What's good merely for General Motors can flush itself down the drain — we want what's good for Money itself. "Flash" investments are now carried out in nano-seconds by computer. Humans are no longer involved (except to scoop up the chips.) Money begets money; no midwife is required.

At a conservative estimate, ten times more money "exists" than it would take to buy *everything in the world*. Some say more, much more. What mangy cigar factory can compete with such alchemy? All Money is *fiat* money. Money is the best proof that magic works — it's pure imagination, pure belief ("credit"), pure bullshit — and yet it has become our highest and indeed our only form of "value". I call this penumbra of money the Numisphere — it englobes the globe like some malignant weather condition. I call money itself the Sexuality of the Dead, because it's dead and yet it reproduces itself. Money is cancer.

The Satanic Mill has not vanished — it has merely become an Invisible Empire (like the Ku Klux Klan). You can't see it, because it went away, far away, and yet it lives *in us*, in each and every one of us, as we use up 70% of the world's resources to stuff 20% of the world's population with junk food and cultural pap, while 1% of the population sits on 80% of the world's money. What do they do with it, one wonders. Croon over it like Uncle Scrooge? Bathe in it?

In this situation all hope of reform becomes sheer nonsense, never mind any talk of utopia. Neo-liberalism, after all, represents the highest type of world evolution — so how can it be reformed? Any talk of change smacks of (gasp) socialism — that dinosaur ideology of yesteryear, the bad old days of welfare and sharing and free healthcare. Or even worse — of anarchy.

In any case, who actually rules us? Whom could we *kill* and thereby reform the world? Lawyers? Bankers? Politicians? Scientists? Educators? Police? Just suggesting it reveals how silly the idea of "revolution" has become. Millions of underemployed and desperate clowns are chomping at the bit, waiting for their chance to replace any dead Masters of the Universe. The French proved that the Terror doesn't work — you simply cannot cut off enough heads to change reality. There aren't enough lampposts and not enough priests' guts with which to string up all the investment bankers. And it doesn't seem likely they'll listen to our pleas for peace and justice and quit their jobs and take their savings and move to Costa Rica and lie around on the beach getting a tan while "we" set about re-organizing Civilization itself — after 6000 years of class warfare, hegemony, usury, human sacrifice ("war") and slavery ("peace"). And so . . . so much for utopia — for any new "Jerusalem".

**

But wait. The world is going to be saved after all — by nano -technology. Little molecular machines are going to be injected into trees and frogs and rocks and your bloodstream and even your brain — so in the future all you'll have to do is *think* of something to buy and it will at once appear before you. Aladdin's lamp! No more clumsy cellphones — there'll be *artificial telepathy*. And no more automobile accidents — cars are already *intelligent* and drive themselves and never drink or do drugs. Everything will appear green because the satanic mills will all be *virtual*. They'll be *inside* you. Just as Stewart Brand predicted in 1968, the "personal" computer has allowed us all to work at home and have compost toilets. Nuclear power will save us from fossil fuels and global warming — and nanotech will cure Alzheimer's and cancer and schizophrenia.

But wait. Didn't I say that we're already living in the Future? True, we don't have any leisure (in fact less than in the fucking Dark Ages) and we don't all have personal ornithopters and robots to mop the floor and scrub the toilet. We're still sick and sad. But History came to an End so this *must* be the Future. Nevertheless, maybe the Future itself has a future, and it's the final heaven on earth promised by nanotechnology. At last. And not a moment too soon!

Recently I heard that in Mexico, of all places, a terrorist group is now emulating the Unabomber and threatening to kill . . . nanotechnology scientists. They claim to be Anti-Civilization anarchists and call themselves "Individuals Tending Toward The Wild" (or literally "the savage"). They admit that their project will not change the world, but say they want *revenge*. (I guess you could call it pre-emptive revenge.) But don't fret. So far they've only managed to kill one nanotechnologist.

If the Future has a future, does the End of the World have an end? Some of ye now living may see it come. The Harmonic Convergence. The Mayan Apocalypse (which has been re-scheduled from 2012 to 2018). Armageddon. Ragnarök. Or maybe — worst of all — eternity in the form of an infinite on-line shopping mall. No closure. No rapture. Just Facebook and Twitter — forever.

III

Up till the middle of the twentieth century the official history of science treated alchemy and other Hermetic "arts" simply as failed science, outdated superstition, evidence of a long Dark Age finally dissipated by Newton's "let there be light", proof of the *ur-dumheit* of all ancient humans, from the nasty brutish short cavemen to the deluded black magicians of the Renaissance.

The ironic aspect of this perspective was of course that Newton himself practiced alchemy and smuggled the qualitative Hermetic notion of action-at-a-distance into the quantitative theory of gravity. He published nothing of his alchemical or Hermetic work, however, and thus the historians (who never bothered to read his unpublished alchemical works) were free to erect their fantasy of a Scientific Enlightenment, with a giant Newton sweeping away the cobwebby shadows of medieval trumpery and suddenly giving birth to the uneasy marriage between empiricism and rationalism.

At Newton's elbow his trusty sidekicks like Robert Boyle and the savants of the Royal Society all chipped in to the revolutionary effort, and soon the Modern Age was born, and "we" appeared on the scene, blessed by perfect hindsight with which to denigrate the Past and its foolish avatars — "we", fully evolved humans, on the verge of discovering the Grand Unified Theory of Everything and inaugurating the scientific heaven on earth — the Great Instauration.

This cozy self-congratulatory haze was however threatened, first by C.G. Jung, who suggested that alchemy might have to be taken seriously as psychology — and then by the brilliant Frances Yates, who first seriously proposed the notion that alchemy was simply *early modern science*, and that the "shoulders" Newton stood on had been those of the Hermeticists.

In 1972 Betty Dobbs published her shocking *Search for the Green Lion,* a study of Newton's alchemical manuscripts. And even more recently the scholars L.M Principe and W.R. Newman have revealed that Boyle was also an alchemist, and secretly lifted many of his best ideas from his guru, American alchemist Richard Starkey ("Eugenius Philalethes"). Principe has propounded the idea that alchemy was not only Early Modern Science, but actually uncovered a great many scientific truths. The earlier historians of science had grudgingly admitted that some Hermeticists might have stumbled on a few facts by sheer accident, but Principe has gone so far as to replicate certain "spagyric" experiments with amazing success.

At the same time — i.e., the twentieth century — an opposing school of thought about Hermeticism emerged from a Traditionalist or religious perspective, claiming that alchemy was never meant to be "scientific" in the modern sense — not even "psychological" — but *spiritual.* One of the more intelligent proponents of this theory was the Swiss Sufi Titus Burckhardt. Almost no one however managed to wrap their heads around the possibility that alchemy might be *both* spiritual *and* material, that the laboratory was also the oratory, that work on herbs and metals was precisely and mystically analogous to or *symbolic* of work on the self. Aside from Mircea Eliade, the Historian of Religion, probably the leading exponent of this view, the mysterious Fulcanelli (author of *The Mysteries of the Cathedrals*), was ignored by both the scientists and the Traditionalists. (Recently it has been argued that "Fulcanelli" was in fact a team made up of at least one practicing "operator of metals"— and a theorist, said to have been R. Schwaller de Lubicz, who later took up Egyptology.)

Erasmus Darwin's Hermetic enthusiasm was not confined simply to the deployment of Paracelsan Nature Elementals as "characters" in *The Botanic Garden*. A true proto-Romantic (and big influence on Percy and Mary Shelley), he sought to integrate a rectified Hermetic worldview with the best contemporary biological science. (His hero Linnaeus did the same, although he's not usually given credit for it.) Darwin developed what might well be called a Romantic Theory of Evolution, partly Lamarckian but largely original, in which all species "descend" from an original unicellular plant/animal like Hesiod's Chaos, symbolized in alchemy as an *egg*. *Selection* (though he didn't use the term) was seen as sexual and based on desire and pleasure. Darwin believed that flowers could *become* butterflies. In meditating on the "White Cliffs of Dover", which are vast repositories of sea-shells, he imagined all the *jouissance* involved in so many æons of reproduction, and spoke of evolution as "the survival of the happiest". His grandson Charles Darwin's sidekick H. Spencer perverted this charming idea into *"survival of the fittest"* and used it as a pseudo-scientific underpinning for "Social Darwinism" — ideological camouflage for classist/racist imperialist triumphalism: — the poor are the *unfit*. Charles Darwin's cousin Francis Galton took this theory a step further and invented *eugenics*, the "science" which proposed eliminating the unfit (and racial mongrels) by preventing them from reproducing. This racism was adopted with terrifying enthusiasm by "scientists" in America and eventually by . . . Hitler.

So — can we say that Hermeticism gave rise to the "modern science" of genetics, which is of course merely a rectified version of eugenics? (Genetics is more accurate than Nazi science, but the social implications are nearly as dire. In the Future only the poor will be ugly and queer.) Yes — Hermeticism deserves some credit — and some blame (for its "Prometheanism"); it's also possible to imagine a world in which Hermeticism was never stripped of its essential insight, that *the earth itself is alive*. Romantic science could have given rise to a contemporary science based (like Rosicrucianism) on the ethic of service to humanity and preservation of Nature, instead of service to Capitalism at the expense of the environment.

The Royal Society was founded by Whig Freemasons (of the London Grand Lodge) whose idealism was wrapped up in Enlightenment values and Imperialist ambitions. Opposed to them were the Jacobite "Ancient" Masons of the Scottish Rite, and other esoteric lodges devoted to Templar chivalry and Rosicrucian alchemical pursuits[2].

The few historians who have paid any attention at all to Freemasonry (a dangerous tar baby for any academic reputation) usually assume that the "Liberal Whigs" are the good guys, and the "reactionary Jacobites" are the villains. It's not so simple, to put it mildly. The Whigs, backed by the British Empire and nascent Capitalism, went on to turn "liberalism" into economic oppression and science into "the cruel instrumentality of Reason". They eventually abandoned all occultism and Romanticism for a pure Newtonian rationality that would lead, step by step, to Hiroshima and global warming — not to mention WW I, WW II, WW III and the endless war of American neo-liberal neo-imperialism, all based on *Technopathocracy,* the scientific rule of sick machines.

The Jacobites, who in principle were monarchist traditionalists, underwent in practice a strange metamorphosis: they became the underdogs, the old moles, the eternal revolutionary opposition. A weird phenomenon unnoticed by official history gradually took shape. I call it "Leftwing Jacobitism" — a shady conspiratorial underground of feckless cavaliers, Non-Juring Anglicans, Irish and Scots rebels, malcontents, pirates, poets — and alchemists.

When Whigs turn into people like Herbert Spencer, and Jacobites turn into people like Robert Burns, we can say the world's

---

2 See M. Schuchard's great book on Swedenborg for the complete story.

turned upside down indeed. Paradox? Yes. So what. Is there a "hidden wisdom" to be found on the side of esoteric Jacobitism in the paradigm war for modern science? Yes — and it's too bad the Jacobites lost the battle.

The "arrows of desire" and the "chariot of fire" were defeated. Blake was defeated. The anarchist movement was defeated. Alchemy was defeated. Newton won — and he did it by stealing the fire of alchemy.

**

German *Naturphilosophie* and British "Sacred Theory of Earth" — the proposals of Novalis and Goethe, Erasmus Darwin: — once upon a time these ideas seemed to stand a chance of being taken seriously as scientific hypotheses. They were opposed by a Victorian vulgar materialist scientism that spoke of the world as *Nothing But,* as in "nothing but dead matter", illuminated only by the *Cogito* of the scientist. "Nothing but" sheer accident gave rise to life, which obviously will vanish at last according to the Second LAW of thermodynamics — the most evil and depressing scientific idea ever propounded — thankfully now losing its hegemonic and suffocating legal status — at least in certain radical circles. Quantum, Chaos, and Complexity theory once seemed to open up once again the possibility of a Romantic science[3] — although the Whigs are still at work debunking all such fond hopes. Chaos they say is a deterministic science — useful perhaps for predicting the stock market. Quantum physics will lead to bigger and better bombs — and as for life, it will be created in a laboratory any day now. (The evil genomist Craig Venter claims ridiculously to have done it already.)

For years I've been saying that the true Science Fiction writers who accurately foretold the Future we now inhabit were P.K. Dick and J.G. Ballard. Read *Ubik.* Read *Crash.* I call their insight "Malthusian Gnosticism". It's the death of the Social. It's

---

3 *The Dancing Wu Li Masters,* for instance (1979)

Bladerunner, *The Drowned World* — it's Frankenstein's World — it's Nietzsche's Terminal Humanity. It's the End of Theory.

IV

What would science be like today if the State had never emerged?

Imagine that 6000 years ago the people of Sumer had successfully resisted the *coup d'état* carried out by evil priests and warriors, resisted hegemony and separation, refused Work and Debt and Slavery and human sacrifice. After all, as P. Clastres pointed out, pre-historic people were neither "good" by nature, nor were they stupid — they always knew that bullies could take over the tribe if they were allowed to, and "old customs" were created to prevent them. Potlach, reciprocity and the "economy of the Gift" were reinforced by tradition. Shamans and war-leaders who threatened to take power were ignored or killed.

But then, circa 4000 BC, something went wrong, very wrong, and the bullies finally prevailed. The Old Stone Age regime of rough egalitarianism and the taboo on tyranny was overthrown by a new elite with a new set of violent patriarchal deities: Moloch and Mammon, War and Wealth. The Shamans (most of them anyway) allowed themselves to be turned into priests, and prostituted their *scientific knowledge* to the newly-emergent State in return for a share of power and riches.

It wasn't the Industrial Revolution yet — it wasn't Capitalism as we know it — but it was a start. Metallurgy and writing were invented as technologies of control. A class of fellahin was created to slog and sweat for the glorious rulers. High Culture (so dear to historians and archeologists) arose on the backs of debt-ridden peons and miserable slaves. In short, the Modern World — *our* world — appeared. Progress appeared. And science was its most loyal servant.

In theory, this debacle or *dégringolade* ("tumble") need never have occurred. Humans could have remained in a condition of "primeval anarchy" without the State, and yet still possessed a true science. The shamans might have presided over a body of knowledge devoted to Humanity and Nature rather than power and wealth. Society might have retained its non-authoritarian structure and yet still increased in wisdom — in good medicine — in harmonious reciprocity with forests and animals — in psychological health and spiritual realization. "Progress" was never written into our genes, it was never evolutionarily determined, it was not inevitable. In fact, Progress stopped our real evolution dead in its tracks — it prevented us from *becoming* what we *are* (to paraphrase Nietzsche) and instead reduced us to Masters and Slaves. And science served as the midwife of this abortion. We learned how to build pyramids rather than . . . what? We'll never know what we *might* have created, if the State had never emerged. It's too late.

The hunters and gatherers changed over to an economy based on horticulture and animal domestication. With hindsight we can understand that this was a Big Mistake. Diet degenerated, chronic diseases appeared, freedoms were eroded, Work was invented. Historians and archæologists call this the Neolithic Revolution and see it as the real beginning of Progress.

Even now however the State does not emerge. The old customs remain strong enough to resist separation and hegemony. The stored surplus is shared, not monopolized. Even Megalithic architecture can be created by egalitarian societies with plenty of leisure and a desire to manifest beauty — no slaves are necessary to built Stonehenge and Newgrange, or even Göbekli Tepe. The unit of society is the village, not the city; the Temple is simply the heart of the village, not the Holy Bank of Sumer, lending silver at 33⅓% compounded annually, or planning a war of extermination against its nearest neighbors. Even metallurgy — as Eliade points out — has a holy origin and in fact can be seen as proto-alchemy. Only with the emergence of the State does metal become the technology of death. (All "primitive peoples" reject metallurgy, from the Irish Tuatha Dé Danaan to the North American woodland Indians: metal is seen as blasphemy against Mother Earth.)

Indulging in speculation about a science of the free spirit may add up to nothing but a bit of "science fiction" — but after the ghastly 20th century and its obvious failure to provide the utopia promised by optimists of the 19th, a critique of science and technology began to emerge, not only from a few eccentric scientists, but even from sociologists and historians of science. Thomas Kuhn for example demonstrated that the development of science cannot simply be charted as a unilinear "progress", but consists of a dialectic series of "paradigms" that are to some extent socially determined. The great Paul Feyerabend [*Against Method: Outline of an Anarchist Theory of Knowledge*] took a similar argument to radical lengths and dared to accuse science of philosophical incoherence and social irresponsibility—unfortunately, however, his work, unlike Kuhn's, has failed to attain canonical status.

Meanwhile a series of archæologists and anthropologists began to question the dogma of Progress and look more carefully at actual evidence. M. Sahlins, P. Clastres, E. Richard Sorenson, and their colleagues in the 1960s and 70s proposed that hunter/gatherer and horticultural societies, far from living in a condition of "war of all against all", appear remarkably peaceful compared to Civilization; and that far from endless toil for an inadequate return they were "original leisure societies" blessed with abundance. By projecting this view back on pre-history, it became obvious to these thinkers that the Paleolithic had been misrepresented by apologists for hegemony as a period of violence and penury, whereas it appeared to an unprejudiced view as based on egalitarian "mutual aid" and tribal "original anarchism".

In this respect, P. Kropotkin and C. Fourier were better social scientists than Spencer or Marx. The Situationists and certain anarchists (such as F. Perlman of "Black & Red") began to develop a critique of Civilization that owed a great deal to the Romantics and the later (post-Leninist) Surrealists. Thinkers like Benjamin, Breton, Bataille, Bachelard and Corbin carried out a *defense of the Imagination* that provided an æsthetic for the new "primitivism". Later theorists like Foucault, Debord, Baudrillard and Virilio lent their efforts to a critique of power and hegemony that added depth to the philosophy of opposition to Civilization.

Eventually a position emerged that I call *anarchotraditionalism*. Rejecting the Progressivist Left as well as the Reactionary Right, this philosophy calls in equal measure for a *Reversion* or "return" of the Paleolithic (at least on a psychic level) and a "revolution" for an anti-authoritarian utopia.

Obviously such a movement would require the overcoming of 6000 years of bad science. "Appropriate technology" (i.e., luddite *techné*) would replace the Satanic Mills of Information Capitalism with a kind of "Green Hermeticism" based on the experience of an *animate Earth*. "Defeated" paradigms such as alchemy would have to be reconsidered and even revived in new forms.

Is such a consummation, however devoutly desired, in any sense possible? Anarchists like to speak of a "Politics of the Impossible", but is this simply a nice way of admitting defeat?

From a purely existentialist p.o.v., it seems necessary to refuse to "cease from Mental Fight" even if there's no reasonable "revolutionary hope" for the utopia of Blake's earthly Jerusalem in "England's" — or the whole world's — "green and pleasant land". The point is not victory, but the struggle itself, which gives meaning to life.

Is even this attenuated vision simply delusory in the face of the Rule of Pure Money and its technopathocracy? Is there any point to hatred of technology and the "critique of science" other than the sour satisfaction of a few acts of revenge?

This is as far as I can go with this *thought-experiment*. I cannot answer the last question.

June, 2014

Medical Hell Realms

Æons ago I worked (as a Conscientious Objector to the War in Vietnam) in three hospitals. The first two — menial kitchen labor — were in Maryland where my Draft Board was located. I was fired from both for insubordination. In the third job, in New York City, at the now-defunct Flower Fifth Avenue teaching hospital on the Upper East Side, I worked as an unskilled lab assistant.

In Baltimore one of my fellow-workers had explained to me that there exist only two kinds of jobs in the world — (a) "gigs", in which one is paid to do what one would do even without being paid (e.g., play jazz); — and (b) — "slaves". "Our jobs here as mopologists", he added, "are 'slaves'."

The NYC position was also a *slave*. My job-description (when anybody asked) was "*mouse-herd*". I took care of a colony of sick experimental mice up on the top floor, the vivisection lab, a setting worthy of a Hammer horror film, with dozens of cats, dogs and monkeys living in Hell — scenes I don't want to remember but can never forget.

As my chief task I killed thousands of unneeded baby mice (killing an adult for scientific use was called "sacrificing"). After leaving that job in 1968 I vowed never to kill another mouse, and have not done so, even when they invaded my shabby cabin in Upstate NY. I'm not a vegetarian and I'm not even exactly a pacifist anymore, but I remain an anti-vivisectionist.

The main lessons I learned from my jobs concerned the nature of being a proletarian in America — an educational experience I never would have had without the War. Ever since then I've avoided "work" as a disguised form of slavery, and I consider that anyone has the "right" to do anything to escape such a fate.

Some years later when I read Ivan Illich's *Medical Nemesis* (a.k.a. *Limits to Medicine*), I also swore to try to give up "medical consciousness". Illich himself pointed out to me when I met him in 1976 that addiction to any "alternate" form of medicine such as traditional healing and the like is no better than addiction to "modern Western medicine". All medical forms merely reinforce addiction to the medicalization of the self. Herbalism could be useful (he thought) inasmuch as it might enable self-prescription, hence freedom from doctors — but the main point was *not to think about being sick* — in other words, not to give in to the cultural obsession with disease under the guise of obsession with the culture of healing. Whether one becomes a "medical object" under the ægis of allopathy or homeopathy or Paracelsan spagyrics or shamanism makes little difference to the soul which sees its body as sick and thus in need of (re)mediation by experts.

Illich concerned himself primarily with freedom from false consciousness; secondarily he refused to spend more on medicine than the average poor Mexican peasant could afford. Of course, Illich was a saint (I mean this literally) so the second ideal might well elude us lesser mortals; still, his first point might at least be allowed to influence our thinking to some degree.

For the next forty years I succeeded in staying away from the iatrogenic disease farms called hospitals as well as the consumer fetishism and psychological dependency of medicine. In recent years however I have at last succumbed — I have become "sick", or rather, have allowed myself to become a medical object. I had a choice — but I am no saint, and I couldn't make that choice. I became old. In Paleolithic hunter/gatherer society I would probably have died although one shouldn't underestimate the power of shamanism. Nevertheless, in former times people often died and were not preserved as medical objects or living mummies. They had only the "life expectancy" of their basic nature-bestowed state of health — or lack thereof.

Note: In the Neolithic, pain was treated with opium — and when symptoms are suppressed the body can often overcome disease. Nowadays our "pain killers" are *less effective* than opium. The dreamy psychotropic effects have been eliminated, leaving only highly addictive synthetics that make you groggy and don't work very well. The poor, as we know, deserve to suffer. Still, one wonders why pain-relief remains such a "primitive" branch of medicine in the modern world.

Nowadays — in this Future we now inhabit — our "life-expectancy" has somewhat improved. In America we often hear triumphalist pæans of medical self-congratulation about our extended longevity thanks to the miracle of modern etc. Of course, if you look at the USA's world ranking in this respect the picture is not so rosy. We come in somewhere between Botswanaland and Spain. It turns out that allowing the insurance and pharmaceutical powers to run our "health plan" is a lot less effective than, say, the pathetic remnants of Social Democracy in Scandinavia or even England. "We" seem quite willing to pay for Permanent War and occasional bank "bail-outs" — but not for our own health or prosperity. We have all the liabilities of "Big Government" and none of the potential advantages. As an anarchist I believe that until the State is abolished, the Government should pay dividends, not collect taxes (except from corporations). But then I'm a crank.

Our "extra" years of life, according to all organs of social propaganda, are supposed to be devoted to happy healthy retirement — maybe a condo in Florida — surrounded by loving grandchildren and superhuman doctors — "free" to go on shopping and playing a vital role in maintaining the Economy of Universal Debt — our golden years — like a free gift from the Spirit of Enlightenment and the instrumentality of Pure Reason.

However, the truth (withheld from us by compliant media) is that these added senior years will be spent by most of us in *being sick*. Death on the installment plan. All the money we saved in a lifetime of 9-to-5 alienated labor can now be spent on doctors and medicine. All the "social security" (unpaid wages) we earned by sacrificing our lives on the altars of Moloch and Mammon can now be turned over to capitalist behemoths in order to enrich Big Banks and Big Insurance companies and Big Hospitals and Big Pharma — all operated for the sole economic benefit of the tiny One Percent.

(Example: as I write this, the new miracle drug to cure hepatitis C costs $1000 per pill. Here in the Future, only the rich and well-insured can afford to be healthy. The poor are with us always — but not for as many "extra" years.)

In America we don't make much of anything anymore — no pencils or shoes or lamps or sweatpants —we sent all that work Elsewhere, to the land of low wages and no unions. We live in a clean pure economy of financial speculation and Information far removed from the stench of mere production. We have illegal immigrants to mow our lawns. But sadly not all of us are smart enough to be data hackers, lawyers or stockbrokers — and there must be jobs for the Others — well, let them work as "care-givers", doctors and nurses, hospital administrators. (Not that doctors are badly paid. But unlike, say, bankers, they really have to work to earn their fabulous life-styles. That's why so many of them are Pakistanis.) Senescence is a growth industry. "Baby boomers" like evil zombies or Struldbrugs outnumber the young and healthy. Undeath has a bright future.

So I've given up. I'm just part of the *situation* now. I'm not going to bore the reader with any "disgusting" details (as William Burroughs used to say) of my "condition". I don't want to speak from *inside* the system. But as an historian I find I have a few remarks to make about the kind of things historians look at in order to "do" history — such as art, architecture, landscape: — æsthetics, mood and emotion.

**

In certain old movies clever directors and set designers used to turn ordinary buildings and "locations" into alien artifacts. Eerie blue light emanating from no discernable source was a perennial favorite. Shadows going the wrong way. Green gray "institutional" paint jobs. Glassy-eyed actors with weird distorted make-up. Gloomy enigmatic signage.

Medical architecture probably has its own professional journals and academic degrees and respected specialists. I'm too tired to do the research. Who needs research anyway? The results are so indisputably *there*.

First one is met with the pretense that everything in Medicaland has been designed to soothe and pacify the consumer, to damp down all panic and angst — but this false cheeriness of course produces the very effect it pretends to cosmeticize out of existence. The bright faux-modern façade does not hide but blazons forth (in heraldic terms) the basic situation — the powerless *patient* in the hands of a robotic bureaucracy. Kafka couldn't improve on the long drawn out miserablistic vistas of the corridors in their sinister "warm" beige and cream tints.

The "art" reproductions on the walls of these corridors are chosen *apparently* for their innocuousness, but in reality their maddening banality achieves a kind of anti-surrealism, a bad-dream-world disguised as sentimental crap. Poor Van Gogh makes frequent appearances. Apparently you're supposed to think of his sunflowers as cheerful, and not as the suicidal icons of despair he really painted.

An art world friend tells me he knows rich collectors who take their own pictures with them when they have to spend time in the hospital. Good art, like say the music of Bach or Ali Akbar Khan might actually expedite healing. In an alternate universe perhaps no anodyne repro-landscapes or photos of cute animals (or pop-schlock music) are permitted in therapeutic zones.

In seeking to monopolize and medicalize the patients' (and workers') consciousness toward a "safe" two-dimensional state of numbness, the art and lighting and rugs and paint jobs and *shapes* of the buildings paradoxically counter-produce existential nausea and sheer terror. But is this really a paradox? Isn't this stuff actually intended to plunge the humans enmeshed in its aura into pits of despair? I mean, on the unconscious level of course. Consciously the effect is meant to be rigid control. Everyone behaves well. Eyes are averted from real suffering. But every *symbolon* in the healthcare milieu is geared toward one message — that you are here to pay to suffer. In between the vapid artworks the staff have taped posters of diseased organs in vivid colors with chipper warnings about dire fates. The soundscape: constant cheery nurse-voices chatter away about inanities — sinister billion-dollar machines emit unceasing digital beeps and hums. Soft pop music filters into the Operating Room. The æsthetics of anesthesia. The *light*: glares: never goes off: never gives way to either day or night. The smell? You know that odor of old, that cold hygienic odorlessness of nothingness.

The building's exterior is designed to look as much as possible like it's not there, so much so of course that it becomes "paradoxically" as heavy as gravity on Jupiter, glaringly obviously *ill*. Critics of architecture speak of "sick buildings". But these buildings are designed to be sick. Their shapes can terrify more effectively than those of any mere Lovecraftian cyclopean ruin or Hitchcockian Victorian mansion in decay because they're so obviously *hiding* their true inwardness — their truth — which is the truth of monopolistic counter-production — the truth of suffering disguised as "healthcare"— of medicine as disease. Or as Blake would say, everything has its *Emanation* and its *Spectre*. Here form is health and the spectre is counter-health. The dialectic grinds to a halt.

Not to mention how cheap and cheesy the architecture appears — no longer the solid melancholy of the 19th century gothic brick temple of death — but the plastic pre-fab designs of a computer geared to save costs and inflate profits, an æsthetic of bottom line infrastructure plastered over with hugely tasteless hi-tech superstructure. Set in a "park" where no one ever plays or strolls or makes love — "nature" without life — *nature morte*.

And in every waiting room huge TVs blast away in the panic-stricken hysterical voices of American consumerism. In every patient's bedroom a TV. So you'll never be bored. Unless of course you find television boring. Or offensive. Or sickening.

I've been using Illich's idea of the "paradoxical counter-productivity of monopolistic institutions" — not really a difficult concept. When an institution founded to do function A becomes a monopoly, it paradoxically turns 180 degrees and begins to produce counter-A, the opposite of A. "Compulsory" education makes you stupid. (See *Deschooling Society*.) And modern capitalist universal medicine makes you sick.

Doctors generally won't give you the alarming statistics on iatrogenic hospital-caused disease. But when I mentioned them to one of my doctors, he admitted that hospitals are not places he recommends his patients spend much time in. Illich's point in *Medical Nemesis* was that modern medicine as a monopoly is inherently iatrogenically diseased *in itself*.

We presume that allopathic medicine really once believed in itself as a science of health. Even today most doctors appear still to believe. We believe that allopathy was not deliberately invented to make humans sick so that doctors could gain more power over human society. But is this true?

Does it matter?

The fact is that the æsthetic of modern medicine creates the opposite of health — it creates sickness. Original intention no longer really plays a role. The origin is *written over* — "inscribed" — with its opposite.

Again we could ask what medicine would be like today if Capitalism had never emerged. Would it resemble certain traditional modes of healing based on "holistic" theories of the body/soul/spirit complex — yet at the same time would it be far more "advanced" than modern medicine in such low-profit areas as public hygiene, prevention of disease, diet, shamanic therapy? Who knows. It's too late to wonder about such utopian concerns. Capitalism is not going to repent and reform itself. In the Future (i.e., now) only the Rich are healthy. The rest of us have healthcare. If we're lucky. If we're not Africans or Peruvians. Socialism might have made a difference, but it's too late now to wonder what or how. Doctors, as Illich saw, have taken the place of priests for us. And money has taken the place of everything else — money is our sacrament. Bela Lugosi used to say "blood is life". Now we say money is life.

"First Kill All The Lawyers"

I confess that back in the '60s I committed some violent revolutionary acts — or rather, I tried to. The bombs didn't go off. I'm glad they didn't, because I hate violence — but in a perverse sort of way I'm not ashamed of trying, because philosophically I feel violence (at least against property) may be justified. Not that it usually accomplishes anything. But revenge is not to be despised. And some times one must do something useless and hopeless if only to assert one's existence. (Gide's "gratuitous action").

George Sorel famously argued that violence must be seized back from the monopoly of the State, and that the "general strike" was a legitimate form of popular violence against authority. In order to emphasize the existential aspect of such an act, he called it a "myth" — i.e., it doesn't matter if it doesn't "work" or is in some sense "unreal". (At least I think that is what he meant — he was not a very clear writer. Let's just say this is what I got out of him, accurate or not.)

I appreciate anarchist pacifism, like that of my late comrade Judith Malina, or Dorothy Day — but although I have opposed all wars waged by States, I cannot bring myself to condemn wars (or armed struggles) carried out against states by anarchists or non-authoritarians.

For example, I support the resistance of the Syrian Kurdish autonomous region (Rojava) against the "Islamic Caliphate" and Turkey and other shit-kicking religious forces. The Kurds have modeled their organization on the Zapatistas and other anarchists, and have been called a "stateless democracy". I'm not crazy about democracy, since I have no desire to be ruled by a majority — but the Kurds are the best secular/social force on the ground in the Middle East, and the only hope for defeating the cosmic evil of Islamic fundamentalism and puritanism — which I hate even more than the "Free Market Democracy" and consumer fetish techno-pathocracy of "the West". (The situation in Syria resembles that of the Spanish Civil War — the Kurdish region resembles anarchist Catalonia, and deserves our full support.)

The question I want to ask — not answer — concerns the possibility of the tactic of violence against the second of the two above-mentioned evils — namely the cacatopia of American materialism, selfish greed, money worship, distraction culture, ugliness and death.

During the French Revolution an attempt was made to eliminate the class and ideological enemies of freedom. We call it the Terror, and nowadays it would be difficult to find any sane thinker to defend it. Of course it failed, which certainly contributed very little toward its popularity. But let me play the *diaboli advocatus* here and ask — how was the Revolution supposed to deal with its internal enemies? Beg them politely all to emigrate?

During the Munich anarchist Soviet of 1918-19, the head of the Soviet Army (and expressionist playwright) Ernst Toller used to ask all his prisoners-of-war to swear an oath not to take up arms again against the Soviet — and then he let them go. Naturally, they promptly went off and joined the proto-fascist Freikorps which later invaded and destroyed the Soviet with such sickening violence. Toller, who escaped, ended by committing suicide in New York City when the Nazis launched WW II.

So . . . what about the bankers, billionaires, technocrats, CEOs, corporate lawyers, government scientists, real-estate developers, earth-polluters, species-killers, political lackeys of the Money Power, fundamentalist assholes and other "class enemies" and bourgeois scum who are destroying the universe in the name of Moloch and Mammon?

We post-moderns have all renounced "senseless" revolutionary violence. *The Nation* magazine is currently on a rampage against the "idiotic" revolutionary violence of the '60s and '70s. We have no "revolutionary hope" in any violent solution to the "crisis" of the end of the world. We in the civilized West are all pacifists now (except for our governments, who are allowed to go on killing the usual sacrificial hecatombs of "foreigners" — and our police, who are allowed to kill us).

We could of course go to the Bankers and suggest they "change their consciousness" — via some New Age claptrap or spontaneous metanoia. Take their money and retire to a nice beach in Costa Rica, leaving us on the legendary level playing field of Free Market fantasy to start up human society again *ex nihilo*. In fact most "reforms" advocated by bien-pensant liberals amount to no more than this. Niceness is all. One percent of the babies shouldn't take 99% of all the toys — it's *unfair*. Gosh, why can't they *understand?*

Let us, just for a moment, think the unthinkable. Instead of waiting nicely for the Masters of the Universe to kill and enslave us, let's entertain the notion of killing some of them first. First, the lawyers, as Shaxpur put it. Last hedgefundista from the lamppost with guts of last nanotechnologist. Or anyway enough of them to *encourager les autres* (to leave perhaps for that beach in Costa Rica or wherever). It's simply not true, as liberals always claim, that terrorism accomplishes nothing. Terrorism founded the Republic of Eire, and Israel, and for that matter the fucking "Islamic State" of the Dajjal ("Antichrist"), which nothing seems able to stop from its destined metastasis. [Note: Written in 2015]

Or if we're too squeamish for that, why should we renounce violence against property out of some false morality or mere cowardice? Automobiles are destroying the world — doesn't it make sense to sabotage them? Sugar in gas tank? Molotov in the parking lot? Answer: there are "green anarchists" serving forty years for scratching the paint on an SUV. Car-o-cide in America is a crime more severely punished than murder. It's true *lèse majesté* — because infernal combustion is our real king.

And imagine smashing computers and iPhones. You'd be crucified, like that "idiot" who cast the usurers out of the Temple. And since he failed to reappear "while some of ye yet live", the banksters scuttled right back. It's no accident that banks used to look like temples, even though most are now disguised as take-out fast-food franchises. Blow up a bank? That would be blasphemy — because Money is our God, as that anarchist, "Jerusalem Slim", learned at last to his sorrow. Money rules and money can't be killed because it's already *Dead*. So, as everyone always tells me at this point in the argument, the Unabomber's plan is futile because for every bastard you blow up there's a dozen more eager to take their place. Hey, jobs are scare — except for robots. *Apres nous le deluge,* maybe, but at least we'll have our three cars, our Harvard education, our stock portfolios, our Peruvian nannies and gardeners, our weapons industry, our gluten-free organic gourmet groceries, our sweet *usura* and our delicious hate and disdain for the losers, the schlubs, *hoi polloi*. Who are "these people", these debtors, these welfare bums? Let our police deal with them: a chokehold on the windpipe of the whole world forever.

One possible answer to this counsel of despair might be a senseless act of violence, with no hope of "changing the world" — just to create oneself as an authentic human being.

Millions of people around the world now hate and fear Capitalism and its "superpower" and its bogus zombie kultur, and are ready to die for their hatred. Because the Historical Movement of the Social is moribund, maybe extinct, the only "causes" that remain open to these haters appear to be religious fundamentalism, xenophobic neo-nationalism, racist reaction or nihilism. One can sympathize with their plight — feel sorry for their sickness — without wanting to share it. But let's be clear, at least, about one thing: We also hate. We are not on the side of the technopathocracy and its apotheosis of ennui and usury. We cannot shed any crocodile tears for "our boys in Afghanistan" or Iraq or wherever "we" are currently protecting the interests of oil cartels and international banks. We cannot pretend to be shocked when cops are killed in revenge. Why have they invaded our world with their weapons and sneering arrogance, these flunkies of the bourgeoisie? To hell with them.

I am not *advocating* violence. I'm simply trying to understand it. Personally I prefer Dorothy Day — but I can't follow her example either. I'm confused, and moreover I'm old and sick and beyond any capability for action. But I won't use my debility as a false front for morality. I'm compelled to ask these questions. To whom does violence belong? What does it mean?

The Decay of Crime

The collapse of the crime rate in the USA and Europe constitutes a real mystery. The politicians and police chiefs who boastfully take credit for it must be secretly even more baffled than the rest of us. Stop-&-frisk, broken windows, quality of life, pre-emptive arrest of potential criminals (i.e., racial enemies), and even murder — all these tactics appear as mere symptoms of the same underlying force that's causing the drop in crime itself. But what IS that force? Who knows?

I decided to use a sort of crude Nietzschean analysis of the phenomenon and see if I could make any headway in solving the conundrum. I assume for the sake of argument that at least some modern crime represents a kind of *will to power* or to "expression", and a way of attempting to construct an authentic self *against* the ersatz civilization of conformity and terror.

As a technique for achieving this expression, crime of course frequently proves inadequate and even counter-productive. All too often crime proceeds not from the will to overcome but from an unconscious capitulation to the alien power of authority: secretly one wills to fail, to be caught and punished. This very failure can exercise a glamour of its own. To be recognized as a criminal seems to provide a kind of counter-power — a tragic fate, an exceptionalism, a dandyism of despair, an existentialist nihilism with romantic implications — perhaps a simulacrum of an authentic self.

Nevertheless, a *successful* crime, as Nietzsche pointed out, can at least provide a means to test and strengthen the will, to over-come pretty restrictive laws meant for the herd, for mental slaves and "last men". In this respect, then, a decline in the crime rate must be seen as indicative of a decline in the will to power. Will itself has sickened and is flickering out. Americans have become so inert they can't even rise to petty crime.

Well, as with many of Nietzsche's notions, there's an aspect of the absurd in this thesis — but let's ignore that and again accept it for the sake of argument. *Why* has the will to power collapsed?

An egregious smiley-face idiot named Steven Pinker takes credit on behalf of — the Enlightenment! *Enlightenment Now: A manifesto for science, reason, humanism and progress*, his new book, presents statistical proof not only that crime is down but also that war is vanishing along with poverty & even death.

"The better angels of our nature" (title of his previous book) have allowed reason to prevail at last , after a million years of horrid barbarism, violence, burglary, & rape. Finally evolution has kicked in. Too bad for our ancestors! — but lucky for us, eh?

Never mind the wars in Syria, Afghanistan, Ukraine or Yemen — far-away & unimportant places where marvelous drones allow us civilized people to live & thrive while the last enemies of Progress bite the dust. Science will solve the few remaining problems like climate change way before it's "too late". So — rejoice. Kick back, pop a Xanax, binge on Netflix. Send out for some gluten-free pizza & organic soda pop. Reality is your whore.

Since I too am a pundit I thought I'd offer my own theory on the drop in the crime rate. I notice that it more-or-less coincides with the triumph of the internet & "Social Media". Coincidence?

Long ago the Baroness Lady Margaret Thatcher famously said, "There's no such thing as *society*". At the time some people reacted in rage — but as it turned out, she was *going to be* correct, in the future. And the Future is Now.

There *used* to exist such a thing as the Human Social, if only a few failing remnants. We still imagine there must persist (somewhere somehow) a Social because we see representations of it on TV and other media. And we have *Social Media*, don't we?

Precisely — we have mediated sociality. Presence, friend-ship, conviviality, co-sensuality, even neighborliness, have been *replaced* — by Facebook Twitter zombies with iPhones, earbuds, driverless cars & robots, spaceships to Mars, weedwhackers, Amazon... Nietzsche's "Terminal Human" is the human at the terminal. Now when we say "keep in touch" we mean (Orwellianly) just the opposite: stay far away — text me. According to recent polls even sex is vanishing, being replaced by on-line shopping & suicide. Love, it turns out, was just a kind of Late Colonialism.

My point? Crime demands a minimal will to power — a sort of energy. Our universal fade-out into *representation* has left us etiolated, flaccid. Impotent.

Crime, it seems, was the dark aspect of the Social. (Of course it also channeled some of the frustrated genius of the poor & oppressed — i.e., it was *anti-social*.) In the absence of the Social, it stands to reason, crime must "decline" and even disappear.

Remember 1995, the "Year of the Internet", the moment when we all realized that the Future had arrived at last, that we'd made it, that the Singularity was occurring, that machines were *taking over*? (Of course, as I've often remarked, "artificial intelligence" is a moronic oxymoron. Machines didn't get smarter. Humans got *stupider*. With a sigh of relief we abdicated critical intelligence and handed over the controls to algorithms, robots, and drones. And became the serfs of our own technology.)

Clearly, Big Changes were occurring in those distant days. Clearly, the Decline of Crime must be related to those changes. But how?

On the level of the collective unconscious (if I can use that term in a rough non-Jungian sense) the end of the Movement of the Social suggests and seems to coincide with a kind of "end of the world". The eternal rule of money and technopathocracy strikes the secret soul as simply Hell on Earth. "No Future", as the punks used to say, doesn't appeal to the psyche as an unending festival of consumerist bliss, but as a kind of soft ragnarök, a dull apocalypse, a stupid eschaton, a malignant but boring fate, like TV re-runs in a dentist's waiting-room *forever*.

We now discuss the end of the world — by climate destruction, pollution, nuclear "holocaust", global accident, anthropocene obscenity, resource depletion, super-plague, etc., etc., — as if discussing the weather — i.e., everyone talks, no one does anything about it. Oh, the intellectuals have lots of suggestions — like, write to your congressmen, take up yoga, emigrate to Mars, eat local, change your *consciousness*.

Of course, if we could change our bloody consciousness, the "problem" would at once be solved: the "solution" would at once appear. But we cannot change our consciousness. We're stuck in the human condition. And money itself is making all the decisions, because that's the way it is, that's what nature intended all along: the absolute Rule of Money.

As long as "revolutionary hope" could persist, there still remained the possibility of a shift in consciousness. But we renounced that in order to go "on-line" and "up-load" our consciousness (our *soul*) into the machine. An eternity of debt — that's what we have willed for ourselves. An eternity of slaving for the One Percent (who themselves are just the biggest slaves of Money). The End of the World as universal shopping mall.

So the first discovery we've made about the will to power in the Twenty-First Century is that it's not profitable. Capitalism doesn't like it. Doesn't want it. It must be erased. But something must replace it. What?

If I had to guess, I'd say — *fear*. The chief and characteristic conviction of the anthropocene is *fear*. "Omniphobia" — universal fear.

Nietzsche says that when humans have nothing left to will or express, they become obsessed with self-preservation. The Care (and the Cure) of the self becomes the defining characteristic of the universal bourgeoisie. The "world out there" is seen primarily in terms of its potential threats against our "safety", our comfort and convenience. Our children are too precious to be allowed to — for instance — go outside and indulge in unsupervised play. Cars, disease, predators, the world is nothing but threats. They must stay indoors at their "play stations", their *screens* — they must be trained to live as prostheses of their technology, as consumers, as debtors.

We fear the police — with good reason! — but we find them utterly fascinating. We fear the very machines we adore, as slaves fear masters. Cars and airplanes are our freedom, but also our death. We fear our lawns (full of poisonous insects and weeds). We fear bread — symbol of the body itself. We fear the body — and so give control of it to medical insurance cartels and Big Pharma — keep us sick, but let us linger forever! (like Swift's Struldbrugs, or the withered Sybil in her bottle). We fear sex — STDs, sticky "relationships", alienation, divorce. (Once we believed sex needed to be "liberated" and that it *was liberating* — now we know better.)

We fear the Other — we fear Terror — we torture and murder in order to overcome that Terror, but it persists nevertheless in poisoning our lives. We fear sunshine (cancer). We fear darkness (criminals). We fear rain (acid). We fear the ocean (radiation, toxic waste). Earth, Air, Fire, Water — we fear it all.

We fear the State — not because it wants to kill us, like the old ideological state, or send us to the Gulag (unless we're black)— but because it wants to *help* us, to enmesh us in its bureaucratic bullshit, to bother us, to surveille us for no reason, or for a million reasons, to watch us at every moment. Our bosses too want to watch us at every moment. Are we at our screens, processing our data? *Why not?* GPS will reveal our whereabouts. We will be gently admonished. We might have to be "let go". (Go *where?* Go fuck yourself.)

If we had to *think* about all this fear, it would drive us mad with anger. Unconsciously this has already happened. But we cannot face our madness and anger. So we "internalize" it and bury it. We take drugs for it. We suppress it. We're tranquil now — too tranquil to commit anti-social crimes. Too sedated to express our will to power. Too "busy" to cultivate an authentic self. Too distracted. Too bored.

So here's the logic: the triumph of Capital equals the end of the dialectic. The end of the dialectic means: nowhere to go, no way forward or out or even back. No involvement. This stasis, this paralysis, means: no action, no "meaningful" action such as revolt, no "meaningless" action such as crime. We give up, we surrender, we conform. School, Work, Consume, Die. (But always on the installment plan.) We're too exhausted to sin, much less seek salvation. Life? Let our machines live for us.

And that's my solution to the puzzle of the declining crime rate. It's an hypothesis, and I'd honestly like to see it "falsified" by someone. But I fear it's correct.

Against Sustainability

Recently I've found myself wishing—when I hear the word "sustainability"—that I had a revolver to reach for. "Sustainability" has become a coded mask for a cause I detest—the *salvation of Capitalism*. Obviously, Too-Late Kapital is running down the road to "global" ragnarök, & has been doing so since the great take-off of the Technopathocracy in about 1830 (when, according to H.G. Wells, "the first superfluous human was born")—i.e., the Industrial Revolution, the triumph of the Machine over Nature. Nietzsche dated the birth of the Terminal Human to about this same date; so the first shall be the last.

The whole point of sustainability is to save cars, but re-design them to run on sunshine or salad oil—to save the highways, parking lots, jet planes, suburban lawns, bourgeois yuppie liberal smug self-satisfaction & "first world" entitlement—but to transform them all into something beige, crunchy, "ecological", "organic", smiley-faced, goodygoody—and to go on like this *forever*—"sustainability". To avoid the Fall, even if it means abandoning huge swathes of the human race & its habitat, so as to salvage the part that counts—US—or to put it another way, U.S. (of A.). To escape to Mars with Mr. Musk in a driverless spaceship "shared" by other billionaires, & fuck all hoi polloi & their degraded junkfood "lifestyle".

Solar power & wind power, the panacea of sustainability, are themselves sources of vast hellscapes of æsthetic filth & poisonous pollution — the factories (in Mexico, of course) to produce those ubiquitous alien-grey panels & war-of-the-world-style windmills (impervious to any poor Don Quixote) — to cover the deserts with black glass, the seas with whining avicidal behemoths — so that WE can go on enjoying our horrid health-food, our idiotic iPhones, our crapulous computers, our tedious televisions — not to mention our armies & police forces, our bureaucrats, politicians, lawyers, silicon-valley "disruptors" & all the other parasites & oppressor-class scumbags who take but never give.

Forget sustainability. Forget efficiency. Efficiency is the devil's shit. Fuck "green capitalism" & and its neat corporate cornucopia of consumer garbage & badly-designed "designer" crapola. Technology will not solve the "problems" that technology created in the first place, any more than heroin will cure morphine addiction, or arsenic will save you from arsenic poisoning. The only way to free ourselves from the rule of sick machines is to *smash the machines*. The Luddites saw the light already in 1812. A sledge-hammer is the sole solution.

Late Style

I

Le Décadence

Etiolated. Attenuated. Deliquescent.
Autumnal or even hiemal (hibernal).
Overripe. Decadent. Belated.

I've always felt a predilection for the fragile and over-refined culture of the Late Style. I duly admire great classical thriving civilizations at the height of their potency and purity of style — but I don't really *like* them, I don't feel *at home* in them. But let a place or a people slump into decline, into twilight, into decay, and my soul begins to resonate in harmony.

It's a matter of taste, but not simply taste as opinion or even as sensation — rather, taste as *rasa* as the Javanese say (using a Sanskrit word), or *zauq* as the Iranians say, using an Arabic word. Taste as spiritual / existential experience, *direct* or mystical tasting, æsthetics as identity at the deepest emotional and personal level.

Of course one speaks with respectful genuflections of the Late Style of a Beethoven or a Yeats. "Ripeness is all." But that's not what I mean. I'm talking about *over*-ripeness, actual "noble rot", as the vintners say, a magical decay into sweetness and the nocturnal imaginal.

For instance, in relation to High Renaissance art we could say that Mannerism, the Baroque, the Roccoco[1] are "late" — but not yet late enough for my jaded taste. I like South American and Mexican Baroque, where it begins to look like hallucinogenic folk surrealism, with angels in frockcoats and wigs, and architectural details like spoiled whipped cream or fungus.

---

1 My favorite radio show in the 1960s was "DeKovan Presents", a lisping *précieux* who coined the term "baroccoco."

Mature and deep is fine, but here I intend to praise the senescent and degenerate. The Nazis coined the term *entarte kunst* to denigrate everything they considered unmanly, queer, foreign and anti-Aryan — whereas in fact the objects of their hate were examples of Modernism at its most robust. Nazi art however cannot be called decadent in my sense of the word — it was merely sinister *kitsch*. Does "decadent" mean second or third rate? Not at all. Artists like Moreau and Redon and writers like Huysmans and Wilde can be included under the decadent rubric along with the inferior (but still lovable) effusions of the Salon Rose + Croix or the novels of Sâr Péladan.[2]

The avatar of late 19th century decadence was the Æsthete, the dandy as artist, whether rich or poor, Robert de Montesquiou (rich) or Max Beerbohm (poor). The perfect æsthete does not produce *too much*, only a few slender volumes. From the 1960s (which were rather decadent) I think of Irving Rosenthal's *Sheeper*, the most stoned queer exquisite text since Djuna Barnes's *Nightwood* or something by Ronald Firbank. After *Sheeper*, Rosenthal never published another word. Perfect! Mallarmé wrote very little, and he's the King of Symbolisme. Each œuvre is a perfect enameled flower. His poems calligraphed on ladies' fans can be seen as casebook examples of my thesis.

Some critics seem to believe that Post Modernism has ushered in an era in which every past period and vanished set of values has "returned" and assumed equal validity, or lack of validity, and that no judgments can any longer be made between High and Low, or Serious and Frivolous. But I have the impression that decadence and the Late Style are not nowadays really "P.C." Left-liberals distrust Lateness as a form of reaction (I've seen neo-marxist critics refer to Mallarmé as a "bourgeois æsthete"), and reactionaries distrust it as effeminate, spineless, crypto-anarchist moral turpitude. Damned if you do, damned if you don't. And if you dare admit to a taste for decay you must treat it with irony, as

---

2 He revived the Rosicrucian Order with music by Erik Satie, patronized Symbolist art, and wrote incessantly. He was famous for walking around Paris dressed as a Chaldaean archbishop.

camp, and not take it seriously as art or spiritual beauty. Really, beneath our veneers of PoMo universal tolerance, we live in a strangely neo-puritanical era. If you're queer you must be married, or join the army. Popular media concerns itself with ugly violence, not beautiful eroticism. The erotic is relegated to the realm of mere advertising.

My life was changed (or warped), around the age of twelve or thirteen, by the chance discovery of the Dover Books edition of the drawings of Aubrey Beardsley. I immersed myself in Oscar Wilde and the Mauve Decade.[3] When the '60s rolled around I realized that millions of other isolated teenage Americans had also discovered Art Nouveau and Decadence, and together we created Psychedelic Art and took lots of drugs, like Aleister Crowley. The Fin-de-Siècle was our ideal of the paradise we dreamed of re-creating in order to escape the unspeakable banality and "conformism" of our post-War 1950s childhood. We were decadent and proud. We were *Late*.

II

"Persia"

Persia — not *"Iran"* — was the mental landscape I wanted to inhabit in the 1970s. To be frank, I had no interest in modern Iran, which looked to me like a second-rate imitation of Southern California with really bad politics. So many people wore Western clothes, drove cars, watched TV, etc., that the casual visitor could be excused for believing the country was "spoiled" for the Romantic traveler. That's what I thought myself when I passed through on my way to India in 1968. India, by contrast, fulfilled my expectations (based on Allen Ginsberg and Rudyard Kipling) as a "time machine" for visiting an imagined past. Iran looked colorless and unexotic by comparison.

---

3 Mauve was the first *artificial* color.

In 1971 (thrown out of India and Afghanistan for visa violations) I returned to Iran and actually got a real job for real money — art critic for the English daily *Tehran Journal* — five cents a word! I decided to stay for a while. Soon I discovered that my first superficial impression of the place was wrong. The Past indeed lived on there, but in another country called "Persia". It occupied the same space as Iran and yet existed in another Time.

In Orhan Parmuk's charming book on Istanbul[4] he evokes a very similar situation: the Ottoman Empire, "dead" since 1921, lives on in secret corners, invisible spaces, lost moments, nostalgic atmospheres, the memories of old folks, the crumbling architecture and museumized art, the persistence of classical Ottoman music and even Sufism. This un-dead Past drives Parmuk to despair — and yet he also loves it dearly.

Late Ottoman culture was obsessed by tulips. Everything from tiled buildings to book illuminations to actual gardens pullulated with tulips. Turbans were tied to look like tulips, even gravestones were carved to look like tulips. Religious leaders and aristocrats were painted holding tulips in their hands. Tulipomania had been exported in the 18th century from Turkey to Holland, where huge fortunes were spent on single bulbs, and millionaires ruined themselves trying to breed a *black* tulip.

In Persia, in the 18th century, the Zand Dynasty, centered in Shiraz, fell similarly mad for roses. In 1970 the gardens and pavilions of Shiraz still breathed the rose-scented air of the era, and the old palaces were tiled with roses. Attar of rose — rose-petal jam — Sufi poems about the Nightingale who dies of love for the Rose — books with titles like *The Rosegarden of the Mysteries* — roses became a way of life. What could be more delightfully decadent? And once you got to know Shiraz, even superficially, you realized that in a certain sense Time there had stopped in the Age of Roses. Roses and opium!

The 19th century in Persia, of course was even more Late than the 18th century. Western influence began to creep in, but at

---

4 *Istanbul: Memories and the City,* NY, 2005

first there prevailed what I call the *honeymoon period* of the marriage of East and West. The East takes only what it likes, and transmutes it into its own creation. Only later does the balance shift and the West begin its "conquest" via psychic colonization. Under the Qajar Dynasty in the 19th century a new style emerged that art purists tend to hate because of its bastardized heritage. For example, the Qajar aristocrats wanted full-length mirrors from Europe. They were shipped to ports on the Persian Gulf and then transported to Shiraz, Isfahan and Tehran by camel caravan. Naturally many of them broke. Not to waste the shards however they were sold to tile-makers who used them to create huge decorative displays in the domes of mosques and shrines, and the salons of palaces. The shards were cut and laid out like the facets of diamonds and lit by stained glass windows to create scintillations and coruscating rainbows of light. Vulgar? Yes, totally — but actually literally psychedelic. Magnificent.

The musical equivalent of this mirror architecture arose from a similarly pretentious desire for European grand pianos. The instruments having arrived on camelback it was realized that no one knew how to play them. However, some genius discovered that by using only four fingers, the piano could be played like a *santur*, a kind of traditional hammered dulcimer. I used to listen to this music on an afternoon show on Radio Tehran called *Barg-i-subz*, "The Green Leaf"; the piano sounded exactly like the mirror mosaics looked. Pure light.

In art, Western influence led to a decline in the traditional miniature. Paintings were done in oils and grew bigger and bigger. The Qajar dynastic portraits have a naive self-taught look, but the detail work is meticulous and exquisite — the aristocrats dripping jewels, each hair of their beards beautifully executed. Biggest of all was the "coffeehouse art"[5]: huge panels on rolls of canvas, in a kind of un-funny cartoon-strip format, depicting scenes from Shiite history, especially episodes from the Martyrdom of Imam Husayn

---

5 Coffee had long ago vanished from these cafes and been replaced by tea, but the name stuck.

and his followers: buckets of blood! Itinerant story-tellers would unroll these works in the coffeehouse, and using a pointer, describe the action in poetic and heart-rending rhetoric and streams of tears. From a strict Islamic point of view, this artform was sheer heresy. It's now banned, of course, along with the *Ta'zieh* (Passion Plays) and other popular forms of piety.

The Qajar Dynasty fell in 1907, but its *style* lingered on and provided a great deal of genuine Persian soul culture, even in the 1970s. Shiite extremist sects, tolerated under the Qajar Monarchy, along with Sufism, continued to thrive under the Pahlevis (who needed heterodox religious backing against the hyperorthodox clergy who despised the monarchy). Conservatives saw these remnants of traditional culture as bulwarks against creeping modernism and "west-intoxication" — including the reactionary modernism of the clergy, which is now called Islamism or fundamentalism. Naturally as a hippy I considered this decadent traditionalism to be really *radical*, and I wanted to immerse myself in it.

This taste involved me in hanging around with traditional classical musicians, artists and craftsmen, rug dealers, antiquarians, Sufis, and opium smokers. Opium was the perfect drug for the "Persian" passion, since it induces a *horror vacui* that fills the inner perceptive field with intricate visions of crystalline and vegetative patterns — just like Late Persian art. It also involved, on a social level, lazing around listening to traditional music (most of the older musicians were smokers) and drinking tea.

Even Sufism could involve a similar decadent style. A dervish friend of mine explained that a chief æsthetic virtue in Sufi art, such as singing, was "pain" (*dard*) or melancholy. The proper response to such displayed emotion was to weep. The closest Western equivalent might be seen as the creative melancholia of Renaissance artists (like Dürer) or Hermeticists (like Marsilio Ficino). The same beauty of sadness was transferred, via the Islamic conquest of Spain, by Persian musicians whose legacy lives on today in Spanish music like Flamenco. *Duende*, "spirit", at the highest level of this music, bears a distinct relation to *dard*. I once saw an entire audience of concert-goers in Tehran erupt in wild enthusiasm for a visiting Flamenco troupe from Madrid. "But this is *our* music!" they said.

III

The Last Mughal

India is where I learned to love living in a Late Period. Anything that's ever existed in India over the last 5000 years almost certainly still exists somewhere in some forgotten corner of the land. While I was there in the late '60s some Brahmins actually tried to revive the Vedic Horse Sacrifice, a complex ritual involving years of preparation — but when it came time to kill the horse they couldn't bring themselves to do it. At certain Tantrik and Sufi ceremonies I attended at remote shrines, saddhus and dervishes appeared straight out of Mughal miniatures. It could've been the 16th century — except for the occasional wristwatch or light bulb. It even *smelled* like the Past — sandalwood and rose, dungsmoke, curry, jungle rot, sacrificial blood, burning ghee.

In North India the period that appeared to be still lingering on most noticeably was the Mughal Era. In the South it was medieval Hinduism. In some places it was both at once — and in certain "hill stations" like Darjeeling or Ootacamund, it was both *plus* the British Raj circa 1940. Living in India was like the childhood dream of running away and joining the circus — and in fact in Ootacamund my friend James and I actually did join a circus, a real one-ring circus. He played in the band. I painted posters. In fact, India fulfilled almost every childhood dream. One could see an elephant in the wild, or carrying a jeweled howdah with a maharajah in it. One could smoke hashish with holy men in cemeteries, or opium with gangsters and transvestites in louche O-dens. One could study magic or mysticism or take a siesta in a giant 17th century astronomical observatory that looked like a de Chirico "metaphysical" painting (the Jantar Mantar in Delhi). Live on a houseboat in Benares. Earn your living as a smuggler. Go to the Bombay horseraces in a horse-drawn victoria carriage. And so on.

Was this all exoticism? The post-colonial "gaze" of (mis) appropriation? Hippy self-indulgence? Well, yes and no. In my opinion we were not mere tourists — we were *travelling* — and living — in *difference* — in other places — in a dream, yes — but what's so bad about dreaming? Moreover, since I was a college drop-out, India (and Persia, Afghanistan, Turkey, Morocco and later Taiwan and Java) constituted my true university. "The jewel that never leaves the mine is never polished", says the Persian poet Saadi. Travel in itself can act as a spiritual path.

"Orientalism" deservedly gets a bad rap these days. Most orientalists (especially the Brits) were actually spies. But along with the orientalism of Imperial-Colonial "intelligence" there also exists an orientalism of the *orientals* themselves. All over Persia and India we met people who believed in roses and nightingales, in the Mystic East, in *lux ex oriente*, in traditional beauty. I call this trend *Orientalismo*, in imitation of the 1980s Latin American poets who decided they *liked* being "exotic" and founded a movement called *Tropicalismo*. Somehow the Spanishing of the word strips it of its guilty quality and restores its innocence.

In India the layer of the Past that most engaged me on a psychic level turned out to be the Late Mughal Dynasty. The actual dynasty fell in 1857 after the so-called "Mutiny" (actually an anti-colonial uprising and now called the First War of Independence). The British completely devastated Delhi and attempted to wipe out any last trace of Mughal culture. But they failed.

Before the Uprising the Mughals had already lost their entire empire except for Delhi. Once the richest regime in the world it was now the poorest. Political power had long since been monopolized by the British, and the last Mughal Emperor, Bahadur Shah II, was held a virtual prisoner in the Red Fort. And yet, Mughal culture experienced a strange efflorescence, in fact one of its most brilliant periods, as if wealth and power had evolved or devolved into a kind of poor brilliance, a penniless renaissance, a final Late apotheosis of refinement and perfect taste.

The great arts of the Late Mughal era were all *poor* arts. Some of these arts persisted into the 1970s (and may still persist ...). In the windy season people flew paper kites and held kite duels.

Old men with henna'd beards hung out in perfume shops, smelling the attars for free. Mughal cookery — essentially Persian cuisine with Indian spices — still thrives on the popular level in Old Delhi. (Cooking is always the last vestige of a culture to evaporate.)

Sufism costs nothing except a few *paisa* for the shrine attendants, and Sufism in itself contains a whole culture of poetry, music, gardening, the art of good manners, flower arranging, incense appreciation — all very cheap, or even free.

Bahadur Shah himself was a great connoisseur of elephants, of which he still owned quite a few, and loved to show them off to entertain his people. He was a major expert and connoisseur of mangos. He was a pretty good calligrapher. Since the British bestowed on him a meagre "purse" for royal expenses he was able to carry on patronizing the arts to a certain extent — music and painting for instance, although architecture had to be abandoned as too expensive. (The great buildings of Akbar and Jahangir were melting away into inhabited ruins.) And Bahadur practiced Sufism quite seriously. But above all he patronized poetry and was himself an excellent poet — probably the best emperor-poet who ever wrote. His pen-name was Zafar, and his poetry guru was Ghalib, the greatest poet who ever composed in Urdu, a world-class genius. Ghalib mastered and to some extent also created a style of Persian poetry called "Hindoostani", which is decidedly late, ornate to the point of baroque surrealism, hyper-loaded with metaphor, heavily scented, over the top and quite fabulous (although purists disapprove of it, needless to say, for not being chaste and *classical*). After the "Mutiny" was crushed, Ghalib wrote an account of the sad events in Persian using not a single word of Arabic — to show his disdain for orthodox religion. He was a free thinker, a mystic, and a heretic. The Mughal form of entertainment *par excellence*, the poetry party or *mushaira,* cost nothing at all (except the expense of a few refreshments). The host (often Bahadur himself) invited the best Urdu and Persian poets of Delhi (which included Hindus, women, and even a few eccentric Englishmen), and set the theme, meter and rhyme-scheme for the readings. Held in the cool of an evening, lasting sometimes till dawn, the *mushaira* attained a level of cultural refinement and exquisite æsthetics unsurpassed by any other poetic tradition and totally unimaginable to our own present deprived civilization.

A government without power (or money) can scarcely be called a government. What *was* the Late Mughal Dynasty?

The key to understanding lies, I think, back in the time of Akbar, the most powerful and brilliant of all the Mughals. He had become disillusioned by Orthodox Islam, and decided to create by Imperial *fiat* a new religion that would embrace all the Indian paths and sects, and yet simultaneously transcend them in a kind of *unio mystica*. He and his close advisors (including certain Sufis and Hindu ascetics) began to study all the traditions: not only Islam and Hinduism but Zoroastrianism, Judaism, Christianity, Buddhism, Jainism, and even Chinese spirituality. Together they concocted the *Din Ilahi* or "Divine Faith", and began to practice it.

This heresy more-or-less vanished with Akbar and eventually was overthrown completely by Akbar's own descendent, emperor Aurengzeb, who brought back a puritanical form of Islam. The Din Ilahi went underground, found refuge in certain Sufi orders, and persisted as a *cultural form* or set of memes. When all the panoply of wealth of classical Mughal civilization had fallen away, this culture of tolerance, syncretism, and art still lived on. In fact, losing power actually freed the last Mughals to become something else, something unique — a kingdom of soul. As an anarchist I can't help but admire this state-without-rule, which devoted itself to æsthetic refinement. In fact, while living in North India I began to experience *re-incarnation flashes*, fleeting images of life in the Late Mughal period, so intense they seemed like memories rather than fantasies.

I spoke of melancholy as a creative component of the spiritual path. The Japanese certainly understand the æsthetic value of the poor and sad. In a world where everything strives toward inauthenticity, commercialism, the acute over-hyper-self-consciousness of bourgeois angst, post-modern relativism and irrelevance, sometimes the poor and sad appear as the sole real rare treasures of vanishing culture.[6] But of all vanished and exquisite

---

6 Even in the 1990s I found places in Ireland that had this poor sad beauty.

things surely the Mughal phenomenon is the saddest. It was smashed so ruthlessly by the British Raj that its level of sadness reaches the nakedly tragic. Nostalgia for the Mughals always involves real *pain*. The British spread such vicious propaganda against a people who had simply attempted to free themselves from colonial domination that the legend of Mughal depravity and inhuman cruelty still lives on amongst certain ill-informed historians and tourists. In fact however the real cruelty was perpetrated by Perfidious Albion. From the point of view of the Persians, Chinese and Indians (and Irish), England must be classed as the most evil force in history.

Bahadur Shah Zafar was forced to watch while his sons and grandsons were executed by the victorious English. Then, aged and infirm, he was sent with a few women into exile to distant Burma, where he finally died in Rangoon. The poetry he wrote in this exile, mourning and longing for lost India, now seems like his truly first-rate (even "great") work. Even today in India these poems are remembered and recited. They represent the perfection of "Late Style".[7]

IV

Chinoiserie

I've never been to Mainland China, but I have visited Taiwan and Singapore, which in some respects may remain (I imagine) more old-fashioned than the People's Republic. I've also "done" the Taoist temples and restaurants of San Francisco's old Chinatown, and lived in Manhattan near another great Chinatown for many years. In Taiwan I stayed with a family of Chinese

---

7 For Bahadur Shah and his period see W. Dalrymple's *The Last Mughal* (London, 2006), K. Singh's *Delhi: A Novel* (Penguin India, 1990); Ahmed Ali, *Twilight in Delhi* (1940); also *The Last Mushaira in Delhi* by Farhatullah Beg; and the works of Ghalib.

Moslems; the grandfather, Sulayman Chang, a seventh generation Peking jade merchant who fled the mainland with Chiang Kai Shek, introduced me to Chinese Moslem food (superb) and Taoism, which he himself practiced as a form of yogic meditation. We visited an astounding temple devoted to spirit possession and packed to the roof with antique Taiwanese art. Mostly however I know China through books and museums. Like many anarchists I consider myself a bit of a "philosophical Taoist", and am also an amateur of Chinese tea.

If I owned a time machine I'd certainly go back to the Tang Dynasty, which I came to love through the work of Sinologist Edward Schaeffer. My second choice however would be the Ching (Manchu) Dynasty, the last, which fell in 1911. Once again, it's a question of taste for Late Style — and also of re-incarnation dreams, which I tend to experience whenever I immerse myself in this era via texts and artifacts.

At one point I read up on Manchu shamanism. As "northern barbarians" the Manchus had originally practiced a variant of Siberian shamanism, and when they conquered China and "became" Buddhists or Confucianists or Taoists, they preserved their ancient shamanic practices as well. There was a shamanist temple in Peking — maybe the only shamanist temple anywhere in the world. Shamanism after all is an uncentralized non-dogmatic tribal "primitive" practice, without temples or priests. There's no reason however why shamanism could not become a "religion" and yet not betray its essentially animist-pagan world-view and practice of "spiritual flight". Certain contemporary shamans have suggested that, as an "original religion", their path could evolve as a powerful force for world-wide ecological spirituality.[8]

The "world religions" lost their connection with the Earth Spirit in their yearning for a heaven of bodilessness. But shamanism sees the "Nine Heavens" as prolongations of earth, as subtle forms of matter rather than ethereal immateriality. I explored the implications of this notion in my essay on "The Shamanic Trace" in

---

8 The Kogi of Colombia have also suggested that the world adopt their faith or else face environmental disaster.

Escape from the 19ᵗʰ Century and won't repeat myself here. But I must say that the sheer *strangeness* of the idea of that temple in Peking is one of the magnets that draws me to the Late Manchu period.

In general I'd maintain that there's a certain earthiness in the Chinese popular religious world-view, the level that persists "beneath" the range of the "Three Paths" and in fact constitutes the real spiritual bedrock of Chinese society. The Kitchen God plays a bigger role in old-fashioned Chinese daily life than the Buddha or the Taoist King of Heaven. Chinese alchemy emphasizes a long life *in the body* over any gnostic transports or mystic transmutations. Chinese tea etiquette strikes me as humane and warm compared to the austere and rigid Japanese *Cha No Yu* ceremony. Having persisted in using the same language and writing and eating the same food for at least four thousand years, the Chinese learned how to do everything with elegance and style as well as efficiency (e.g., ideograms, chopsticks). See Needham's *Science and Civilization in China* for innumerable examples. Even when it came to opium smoking the Chinese perfected the technique and created implements of surpassing beauty with which to pursue their vice.

In the case of the Manchus one can speak of a barbarian energy wedded to this immemorial Han practical and æsthetic perfection, a "marriage" that resulted in hybrid vigor. Unfortunately there was also a dark side to the style. For reasons too complex to investigate here, China itself was melting into decadence, a process that was only exacerbated by Manchu arrogance and corruption. Starting with the Opium Wars (and Perfidious Albion again) a series of military disasters exhausted the vitality of the Chinese economy and culture. Of course China's ancient legacy of greatness couldn't be wasted and dissipated in a few brief decades. It remained great — but lost the sense of its own goodness.

This decadence was most exquisitely symbolized in the person of the last Dowager Empress, Chu Hsi, and her gaggle of self-serving crooked Court Eunuchs. A recent biography of the Empress has attempted a defense of her policies, arguing that she made an attempt to "modernize" the Empire without losing its traditional virtues. This is one possible "reading" of the Dragon

Lady. Another would be Backhouse's scurrilous memoir of her reign, now revealed as sheer fantasy, but somehow compelling.[9] The nicest book I've read on the Empress was a memoir by one of her Ladies-in-waiting.[10] This gives a convincing picture of her sweet side, along with such delicious tid-bits as her predilection for adding fresh honeysuckle blossoms to green tea. (I've tried it.)

Æsthetically a certain deep heaviness emanates from Manchu art, furniture and interior decoration, food, music—a sense of stale incense lingering in the folds of shadowy tapestries — a degree of over-refinement and exacerbated hedonics that could lead only to collapse and disaster — which is exactly what it *did* lead to. (See the autobiography of Pu Yi, the last Emperor.[11])

I sensed this heaviness in San Francisco, for instance, in the house of my friend Allison Kennedy, whose grandfather had been captain of a clipper ship, and furnished his home with huge expensive dark ornate pieces of Ching Chinoiserie. I saw the same kind of furniture in the marvelous Dragon Well Teahouse (up the hill from North Beach) where my friend Nick Dorsky first introduced me to the psychotropic effects of *lung ching* tea and afternoon sunlight. On Saturday mornings old Chinese gentlemen bring their caged singing birds to the café for an outing. The ladies who run the place give strict instructions in how to prepare and drink their precious brew.

In Calcutta's Chinatown in 1970 my comrade James and I immersed ourselves in a Chinese opium den for several months. Our fellow smokers were mostly old shopkeepers, who used the den as their retirement club. Fine tea was served. Everyone's good manners would not have disgraced a set of French aristocrats of the 18th century. I consider this experience my deepest immersion in the Ching Dynasty.

---

9 E.T. Backhouse, *China Under the Dowager Empress: Being the History of the Life and Times of Tzu Hsi,* Philadelphia, 1910.
10 Katherine Carl, *With the Empress Dowager of China,* NY, 1907.
11 *The Last Emperor: The Autobiography of Henry Pu Yi,* NY, 2010 (latest edition)

Years ago I read in the *International Herald Tribune* that a group of wealthy Hong Kong businessmen had decided to re-create an Imperial Manchu Banquet. I wish I'd clipped and saved that article, which described an astonishing selection of rare dishes. The banquet lasted for *eleven days*.

The closest I ever got to such an experience was in a Szech-uan restaurant in New York Chinatown which served Camphor Tea-Smoked Duck. The genial waiter was amazed and pleased that a "round-eyed western barbarian" like me could appreciate such a dish. The 100-year-old black eggs served with fresh tofu chilled on ice was also memorable.

V
Late Antiquity

Speaking of time machines again, another prime destina-tion for me would be Late Antiquity — the 5th century AD for example — a taste I share with very few people, it seems.[12] I've written an entire book about it, *The Temple of Perseus at Panopolis*, so here I'll simply note that it's precisely the lateness of the era that appeals to me: the decline of Rome, the decaying Vandals in North Africa, the last dying embers of paganism, the murder of Atilla the Hun, the "Romantic" King Arthur, Egyptian Neo-Platonism and Theurgy. The 5th century to me seems to resemble an obscure run-down foreign city with no spectacular "sights" or famous monuments to attract any hordes of tourists — Surabaya maybe, or Limerick — where the traveler can escape the merely exotic and perhaps contact something real, authentic, poor and sad — some-thing not posing as something else.

The Late Antiquity I'm dealing with in the present essay however is not that of Western "Civilization", which began its decline into progress and emergent Capitalism and Enlightenment

---

12 Except notably G. Traina, author of *428 AD: An Ordinary Year at the End of the Roman Empire*, (Princeton, 2009), a *guide bleu* to that "ordinary" year. Highly recommended.

and crushing boredom – maybe around the 16ᵗʰ century. The Late Past that attracts me lived on in the downtrodden backward undeveloped East (and South). It lasted till the 1960s, when I — as described above — was able to immerse myself in it, occasionally for weeks or even months at a time. Perhaps it lasted only because the colonialist imperialist West repressed all attempts of the East to "modernize" itself. But perhaps it lasted also, at least partly, because some people liked it — eastern people as well as western visitors — because in some ways it was *better* than the "present" with all its spiritual pollution and wars and commodity fetishism and vulgar materialism and ennui.

Was it in fact Napoleon who first discovered the charm of Oriental Lateness? Did he invade Egypt sheerly as a nostalgic Romantic, looking for exoticism to offset the crisis of modernity — which he himself had done so much to inaugurate? Why else did he take all those savants with him to study the history, archæology, sociology, religion and cuisine of that forgotten corner of the world? Was he the pioneer decadent traveler to the East?

Napoleon's botched conquest of Egypt set off another wave of *Egyptomania* such as Europe had been experiencing on and off since the Renaissance. Athanasius Kircher, Piranesi, Cagliostro — these enthusiasts for a land they'd never visited inspired a craze that lasted till at least Mozart's *Magic Flute* — but then Napoleon ignited it once again.

The "orientalist" painter J.-L. Gérôme typifies the French *erotic* attraction to the East. According to one's frame of reference Gérôme's work appears as high camp, as wicked colonialist gazing, or as splendid nostalgism. I think all three points of view are legitimate; in any case he is far from being "two-dimensional". Of course the anti-orientalists and post-colonialists have lambasted art like Gérôme's, which was certainly often tainted by racism and predatory voyeurism. However, once the political miasma has been cleared away to some extent, or at least ignored, it remains true that in some respects the East *was* sexier than the West. Tsk tsk. But there it is.

Capitalism inculcates a weird kind of erotic repression, which has nothing to do with simple sexuality. The Victorians were obsessed with sex but felt they were too repressed really to enjoy it. But once they'd *escaped* from Christian or post-Christian suffocation they blossomed into erotic flowers. Somehow I can't find it in my heart to condemn them utterly. And after all, not all of them were spies or colonial administrators. For some of them their journey into the "past" via the Orient became an initiation into love, into self-realization, or even into political involvement in anti-colonial and anti-racist struggles.

Think for example of the Theosophists. Their love affair with India led them into open collusion with anti-British activists. Think of Roger Casement in Africa and South America — a sexual adventurer who risked his life more than once to denounce colonialist crimes, and who died for the cause of Irish independence.[13]

Think of A. Gide, J. Genet, M. Foucault — all were attracted to the "queer" aspect of eastern culture, and all were staunch upholders of revolutionary tendencies in the countries they visited. (Genet's *Prisoner of Love* expresses my point to perfection.) Oscar Wilde was another erotic traveler who wrote and agitated against European Imperialism and in fact embraced anarchism and socialism.

Gérard de Nerval ought to be canonized as the exemplar of intuitive sympathy for the East. His oriental travel book contains the earliest writing I know which really comprehends Sufism as if from within — which should not surprise us, given his greatness as a Hermeticist and alchemical poet.

Nerval wanted to be an erotic traveler and even went so far as to buy a beautiful slave girl in Egypt. But then he actually fell in love with her and freed her, and paid for her education in a school in Beirut. No "orientalist" was ever less a spy or tourist than Nerval.

In this context we might or might not add Flaubert. Sir R. Burton (*Arabian Nights*, etc.) was in fact a spy, and E.G. Brown (author of *A Year Amongst the Persians* and the magisterial *History of Persian Literature*) might well have been a spy — but both of them truly loved eastern culture and expressed this love in their work.

---

13 See also E. Longford, *A Pilgrimage of Passion: The Life of Wilfrid Scawen Blunt*, (London, 1979)

Perhaps they can be forgiven? In any case, anti-orientalism, for all its virtue, can be seen as all too prone to throw out babies of art with bathwater of politics. Surely both æsthetes and ideologues occupy legitimate bailiwicks?

My own life in the East was shaped by such European savants as Mircea Eliade and Henry Corbin (I knew Corbin in Tehran) as well as by Persian and Indian scholars and mystics I met along the way. Corbin, for one, was adulated by many "native" Shiite sectarians (Ismailis and Shaykhis) and heterodox Sufis as a true *initiate*, not a mere academic. In this sense he might be seen as an avatar of true *Orientalismo*.

Of course the Mystic East, which seemed to promise so much in the '60s and '70s, gradually revealed itself as yet another disappointment. Many oriental gurus who migrated west were unveiled as charlatans or simply blowhards. Even enlightenment itself turned out to be not all it was cracked up to be — it failed to change much of anything, and the Occident continued on its degeneration into materialist squalor and moral hypocrisy. The oriental religions themselves fell prey to fundamentalist and puritan tendencies within their own psychic spheres. Traditional Indian "tolerance", "Persian humanism", and other mystical paths have failed to resist the kind of shit-kicking bigotry that came to characterize (most) Christianity in the West. I blame this situation on the collapse of the Historical Movement of the Social, along with "third world socialism", in the 1990s. People nowadays who yearn to oppose unbridled global-capitalist neo-imperialist triumphalism and coca-colonialism have no recourse or refuge except quasi-fascistic nationalism or religious reaction because "socialism" is dead. For this dire mess the failure of the Mystic East is partly responsible, karmically at least, if not literally.

In fact the "Late" has been supplanted by the Too-Late. The "sixth extinction" is now under weigh and cannot be stopped — for this debacle we can thank "modern science" and "secular humanism". Nothing stands in the way even now of Rat-Bastard-Capitalist cosmic greed, the unbridled rule of Pure Money. The "market" has found ways to profit "obscenely" even from the End of the World. A million *savants* and their books on "green consciousness", "economic reform", and "spiritualization" have accomplished absolutely nothing to prevent this Ragnarök — except create an atmosphere of helpless doom that will merely hasten the day.

Compared with the Future we have now finally come to inhabit, who wouldn't prefer the Past, however beset with darkness and superstition? Nostalgia is now simply a form of brutal realism.

Coda
King Farouk

In 1964 the estate of King Farouk, the "last Pharaoh of Egypt", was broken up and various bits of it were offered for sale even in New York. A rich friend of mine bought one of Farouk's huge hubblebubble waterpipes, a baroque bejeweled monstrosity with six fat scarlet velvet hosepipes. The bowl was so big that it needed an ounce of hashish to fill it. As a result I became interested in that royal rascal.

Around 1975 at the Shiraz Festival of Arts in Iran I met Princess Farida, sister of the Shah's first wife, who had been (if I'm not mistaken) herself a sister of King Farouk; anyway a close relative. According to rumor the Shah had never divorced his first wife (she had proved unable to produce an heir), but kept her hidden away in a palace somewhere out of sight of his second wife, Farah Diba (whom I knew and interviewed several times for various publications). Anyway, Princess Farida was very nice. I gave her a copy of my first book of poems *The Winter Calligraphy*, and she gave me an ivory-inlaid backgammon set, which sadly I lost when I left Iran (in a hurry) in 1979.

Some years later I delivered a paper at a meeting of the Ibn 'Arabi Society in Oxford (later printed in my book *Sacred Drift*, City Lights). In this paper I discussed the growing menace of Islamic fundamentalism, and as a contrast I evoked King Farouk, on the principle that even Late Decadent regimes are often preferable to what comes after them. I described the young debonair Farouk in his perfectly-fitting frock coat, fez rakishly a-tilt, oval cigarette held nonchalantly between fingers; I evoked the old Farouk, ludicrously fat, addicted to pornography and spaghetti (he died in exile in Rome after a gargantuan supper, in the arms of his mistress). I ended by saying, "he was dim, venal, and corrupt — but at least he never attempted to *purify the Faith*."

At this point I heard a single voice in the audience erupt in delighted laughter. It was Bulent Rauf, founder of the Ibn 'Arabi Society, leader of the mystic order of Beshara, descendent of Ibn 'Arabi himself, and closely related to the deposed last Ottoman Sultan. I thought of him as a very serious person and I wondered what I'd said that tickled him.

After I finished my talk he called me over to where he was seated. "Farouk was my cousin. I knew him well. You captured him *perfectly*."

The Empty Screen
(A Short History of Consciousness)

Given that neither science nor philosophy appears to have succeeded in *defining consciousness*, would it prove futile to inquire into its origins and its becoming? Can we even take for granted that consciousness actually exists, and is not merely an epiphenomenon of brain physiology, or even an illusion? In my view such questions fall into the same category as the conundrum of solipsism. Perhaps all that exists is my consciousness, and therefore my consciousness is false if it attributes consciousness to anything but myself. Or perhaps I only think I think. And so on. Yes maybe but who cares? If so then nothing. Let's assume for the sake of this *writing* that everything is as real as it needs to be, and that we are born into an existential or ontological condition commonly known as consciousness.

In short let us accept our feeling, sensation or æsthetic of being conscious, and go on to investigate the nature of such a probable or at least possible state.

Consciousness appears to be more than or different from awareness. Possibly (as the Romantic scientists and Hermeticists believed) even rocks possess awareness, although in another dimension of time practically inaccessible to us — except possibly through alchemy, which would then consist of a means for accelerating the awareness of (the) Stone to the visionary level of consciousness. Certainly plants and animals have awareness; we can, for sake of our discussion, dismiss the Cartesian view of matter as "dead" and animals as insensate machines. The universe, so to speak, is aware. Perhaps the nature of consciousness involves awareness of that awareness. Already we have introduced the metaphor of the mirror (and the myth of Narcissus).

The universe therefore would seem to require consciousness on the part of the perceiving self in order to acquire awareness of its own awareness. "I was a Hidden Treasure", as Allah says, "and I desired (or 'loved') to be known — so I created the world."[1]

---

1 This saying is not found in the Koran or the Canonical Traditions, and may have been "made up" by mystics or even heretics.

If this were so then we could say that consciousness is not an "accident" but plays a real role in evolution — if we define evolution as more or other than the accidental concatenation of insensate matter into a "meaningless" condition we call life. Consciousness could then be seen as the necessary condition for *meaning* or "value" as Nietzsche called it. We could define it as the love (or desire) of the universe for itself.

If this be the case then we must at once ask ourselves the central question of this essay — namely: Why do we find ourselves now facing what might be called a crisis or even a *cata-strophe* of meaning, such that the certainties and symbol-systems of traditional spirituality no longer serve the generality of humanity as bulwarks against the abyss — the "absurd" as Existentialism rather weakly calls it — and the grim denial of meaning on the part of those scientists and philosophers who do not recognize the evolutionary function of consciousness?

We have a sound practical reason for asking the question given that the "vulgar materialist" position has obviously led directly to a condition of modernity based on the reduction of all value to price, and to that triumph of ugliness over beauty we call Civilization. The most revolutionary task that could possibly confront us remains *the giving-back of value to value,* as Nietzsche proposed. But we cannot even begin such an undertaking without first asking, not what consciousness *is,* but what it *does.* And, obviously — where it went wrong, where it began to fail to fulfill its evolutionary function.

**

Our late colleague Terrence McKenna hypothesized that consciousness arose in the moment when a certain monkey ate a magic mushroom. Although I don't literally believe this, I think it's a nice metaphor. An "I-thou" relation between us hominids and the world (in the form of a "sacrament" or holy food) might adequately indicate or symbolize an *origin* for consciousness. Modern philosophy distrusts all origins and pretends to limit its discourse to functions — but we need not confine our inquiries in the straight-jacket of mere positivism. We are not philosophers — thank goddess.

Awareness thus became aware of itself in order to bring about the identification of self and world in a dialectical relation of desire and love. The very moment of separation — in which the conscious "animal" becomes not just aware but conscious of its awareness — is potentially therefore *also* the very moment of (re) union or *unio mystica*, the at-one-ment of self and other.

It strikes me that *language* might constitute the necessary means of such realization, but also and simultaneously the ground on which a failure of consciousness may become possible. Language is perhaps the necessary mirror. But a mirror is already a screen. The universal myths of talking animals (and theriomorphic "gods") already indicate a nostalgia for the undivided self *before language* — the animal self. All "lycanthropic" mysteries of so-called primitive peoples concern this desire for re-integration. Such mysticism ultimately means to overcome language. Is its failure fore-ordained? Is language the original error?

I think we have to exclude this possibility — at least, in order to be able to go on talking about consciousness. Other myths, after all, give primacy to the word, to *logos*: — God creates the world as language, or even as writing. It would be interesting but ultimately not helpful to see language (or even writing) simply as the enemy of some hypothetical "pure" consciousness, since this would amount to a kind of intellectual suicide. Let us accept (at least pro-tem) the notion that our consciousness plays an evolutionary role, and that the expression of this consciousness is the necessary condition for its efficacy.

**

This brings us — conceptually if not strictly chronologically — to the "Paleolithic", to the kinds of speaking humans we call Neanderthal and Cro-Magnon, and to their later *extensions* into time as hunter/gatherer social groups ("tribes"), roughly egalitarian and non-hierarchical, primitive in the sense of primal, original. A number of examples persisted even into historical times and were written about, almost always with prejudice and incomprehension; but at least their existence was recorded. We can use these records to interpret the "past" in which an "earlier" form of consciousness may have existed. In remote corners (or amongst "throw-backs" like mystics and artists) it may still exist. I use the words *past* and *early* in a metaphoric sense, although also in an historical sense. The past could be now. (It isn't even past, as Faulkner quipped.)

What kind of consciousness would differ from ours in such a way that we could recognize it as earlier, as a kind of "dawn", in the poetic terms the *Rig Veda* uses? In order to understand it we must be able to imagine it, and in order to imagine it we must be able to experience it, at least as isolated *satori* moments in which we forget to forget that we and the universe are related. I believe all humans have access to this state, although most of us repress it, for reasons we'll have to investigate. The late Colin Wilson devoted his life to this problem: how to induce and prolong the kind of "peak experiences" in which consciousness works for us, not against us, to restore value and meaning to life.

No doubt I would be accused of shallow exoticism if I were to maintain that "primitive" people have more of this kind of consciousness than we moderns — so let me phrase it in a way that critical theory might be able to accept. Different socio-economic forms of co-existence induce different modes of consciousness. Not even Marxists could deny this. This is the gist of my contention. Thought or consciousness determines the form of life, but the form of life determines thought — or rather the subjective quality of experience and the value of life — i.e., consciousness.

Because of the way in which they produce and reproduce value, primitive and traditional societies may express a deeper and purer form of awareness of being-in-the-world than our highly technologized Civilization usually allows. Excessive economic and technological mediation gets in the way of direct experience. Call it "alienation", to use that term in the sense of Marx's 1844 *Philosophical Notebooks*, or in an Existentialist sense. I don't believe a shaman would see matters very differently — in fact we know that shamanic thinkers from still-persisting "primitive" societies (such as the Hopi or Kogi or Yanomame) have recently made precisely this critique of "modern" or "western"[2] society.

---

2 It seems unfair to blame it on the "West". All three examples I just used are peoples of the western hemisphere. But you know what I mean.

I want to argue, on the basis of archæology, anthropology, art history and history of religion as well as personal experience, that more "backward" societies possess a qualitatively different form of consciousness, less alienated than that of (post) industrial Capitalist society and its monolithic culture of commodity fetishism and vulgar materialism. This "primitive" consciousness seems more attuned to the body, to nature (let's not quibble over terms here) and to a kind of animistic participation-ethos we can associate with "primitive art" and pre-modern cultural styles. I could insert a great many references here, but frankly I believe I've made my point, and I invite readers to immerse themselves in ethnographic literature and replicate my findings (or not). Nobody's paying me for this work, and I'm in no hurry. Footnotes can be supplied by looking at the works of Charles Fourier, A.K. Coomaraswamy, Pierre Clastres, Marshal Sahlins, James C. Scott, Abdullah Öcalan, E. Richard Sorenson, and the "anti-civilization" green anarchists and neo-primitivists like Fredy Perlman and John Zerzan; or see my own previous essays in this area.[3]

My goal here is not to "prove" any contentions about primitive consciousness. I'm taking for granted that earlier and more evolutionary forms of consciousness have been largely supplanted by later counter-evolutionary forms. I want to ask how that happened.

**

Following the theorists mentioned above one can hypothesize that the first big step toward alienation was involved with "domestication" of plants and animals in the Neolithic era in the uplands of what is now Iran, Turkey and Iraq. What probably began as an intensification of a love-relation with certain plants and animals (such that humans desired to live with them full-time

---

3 Such as "The Shamanic Trace" in *Escape from the 19th Century* or the collection of texts called *Ec(o)logues.*

rather than hunt or gather them) resulted in unintended health and consciousness problems — health and consciousness being closely linked (as Nietzsche noted) or "co-creative". No longer "equal" to the plants and animals, as in Paleolithic animism, humans became "superior" to them, as in Neolithic paganism, and then superiority in itself came to constitute a kind of separation or alienation from nature.

Still it must be emphasized that domestication did not give rise to, or inevitably lead to, the emergence of "Civilization" and the State.

The proto-peasant farmer lives a roughly egalitarian communal village life. The temple is the center of redistribution and health, not of debt and "sin". Once the early Neolithic stage of simple gardening and herding is supplanted by *farming* (living fulltime with domesticated plants and animals) the leisure and abundance of the Paleolithic era (which is punctuated by moments of intense effort and occasional starvation) is replaced by a "safer" and steadier economy based on *Surplus*, and on what we might already call *Work*. The former creates anxiety (someone might appropriate the surplus common wealth), the latter creates monotony. (Hunters and gatherers never do only *one* thing.) Worry and boredom erode the "old" consciousness — the result can be detected in Neolithic art, so much less free than Paleolithic art.

But the free farmer lives a holy and cultured life compared to the slaves, the *laboring classes* or fellahin that come into being with the sudden emergence of the State circa 6000 years ago. For a million years humans had evolved to lead a non-authoritarian life based on mutual aid, and now in a flash society turns its back on evolution and re-organizes itself for the exclusive benefit of a *ruling class* of kings, warriors, and priests. The Temple is now the Central Bank, command-center of peonage and repression. All civilizations begin with an orgy of human sacrifice; later this murderous impulse is seen as economically counter-productive and is replaced by war-tribute, slavery, and debt — and ideological religion as the excuse for such misery ("humans were created to serve the gods and the representatives of the gods. To rebel is Sin.")

Ever since then the apologists for power — theologians, philosophers, scientists — have been explaining to us that *Progress* consists of increased wealth and beauty for the ruling class, and harder work and ugliness for the commons. Clearly the "rise" of civilization marks the moment of crisis for consciousness, which must now become *mauvaise conscience*, or "false", in order to maintain the mutual illusion that this unnatural State of being is somehow divinely (or scientifically) pre-determined — that it is actually evolutionary. First (according to the intellectuals) we had universal poverty and war of the Paleolithic — then the brilliant "agricultural revolution" — then the glories of Classical Civilization — at last the ultra perfection of triumphant techno-capitalism. "Darwin" ordained it — so mote it be.

Of course, "everyone knows", in their secret heart of hearts that this is simply not so. Not only did Civilization create injustice and drudgery for us (and leisure and culture for the elite), but it's now clear that Civilization will at last destroy "the environment" (Nature) out of sheer stupidity and greed. The cognitive dissonance between the grandiose claims of Civilization, and the actual banal immiseration of the vast majority of humans, leads either to rebellion, inchoate rage, or to mute despair and consumer fetishism. Religion no longer offers a valid excuse for such schizo-cultural consciousness, and the result is the Future we now inhabit, godless, artificial, ugly, and apparently *terminal*.

This doesn't simply occur overnight. Consciousness has a history. We can trace it in stages from the moment of collapse around 4000 B.C. to the present. But it takes thousands of years for the new economy to spread and infect the whole world, and even today in a few remote backward corners traces of earlier forms of awareness may still persist among tribal or peasant populations. Moreover, over the centuries some humans have always revolted against Civilization— there has always existed an *underground* beneath the surface of oppression and ideology — an eternal secret society or witchcraft or *Tong,* as it were, of refusal and resistance. And of course it's ultimately proven impossible to eradicate the mystics and poets who sometimes see through the mirage and apprehend vestiges of old truths.

Let us attempt to sketch a history of our own consciousness.

**

1. Awareness.
Everything in being is aware.

2. Consciousness.
The Mystery to be solved.

3. Self-consciousness.
Apparently only humans are self-conscious, although one may suspect monkeys, dogs, and even crows. This is the level of language, or the mirror of logos.

4. Tragic self-consciousness.
We become aware of ourselves as tragically and chronically separated from "original nature". We invent spirituality, art and "sexuality" as means of re-unification with the lost world of "animals" (*animism*). Economically this is the stage of the *Gift* — archaic reciprocity; *Shamanism* — mysticism without "religion"; and *Culture* — still without Civilization as the radical separation into high and low "class".

5. Acute self-consciousness.
Here we arrive at the Neolithic, and a certain crisis of consciousness as the vehicle of our deep divorce from "wild nature". The spirituality of re-integration now becomes angst-driven and violent ("sacrifice"), and animism is replaced by paganism. Animism sees everything as holy — paganism projects holiness on the "gods" as *other* than the world. Obviously we have here a spectrum rather than a strict separation between the two attitudes. With paganism the landscape and life itself can "suddenly" be seen as animate and holy — the gods can *erupt* into quotidian existence.

6. Civilized Consciousness.

As Charles Fourier noted, this stage represents the real *fall from grace*. The gods now no longer appear in our awareness, but can only be reached indirectly through mediation ("priestcraft"). One sees oneself as damned, sinful, doomed to Work by a "biblical" curse: body over-written by alienation — body as the *enemy*. Civilization is a mental disease; on a normal planet such people would be treated as insane. Still, we must point out that certain noble forms of consciousness can persist and overcome even the sexual immiseration and "black turnips" of Civilization (as Fourier used to say). The world is not yet felt as "dead matter". Truly great and uplifting art can inspire an æsthetic joy akin to primeval animism — and even the "lower classes" still make and possess such art. Moreover, the early State is still inefficient in its mechanisms of control. Writing may constitute the magic of the State but it can be and is subverted by the eternal underground into a medium of resistance. There still exist unmapped areas of earth to which one can flee and escape one's "masters" ("pirate utopias"). Certain kinds of mysticism and magic lie outside the consensus reality of oppression and boredom.

7. Rationalism.

The gradual apotheosis of Civilization and the emergence of what we can now recognize as Capitalism led to a "Cartesian" Enlightenment which for the first time overthrew the doctrine of the living Earth (which had been maintained by traditional Hermeticism since Antiquity) and replaced it with the dogma of "dead matter" and the isolated *cogito*. The influence of technology and economics may have helped give birth to this world-view, but the world-view itself gave birth to a disastrous new form of consciousness, in which the self convinced itself it was *rational*. Basically this was the moment of the "death of God", although the mournful news didn't quite sink in for a century or two. The result of the sinking-in was Romanticism, which attempted, and is perhaps still attempting, to revive the image of the living earth along with some kind of philosophy and æsthetics of animism.

The new consciousness denies or ignores any "divine eruption" into its life and trains the "cruel instrumentality of Reason"[4] on the world as object (rather than co-subject). Newtonian physics[5] with its clockwork universe is mirrored in economic ideas such as utilitarianism, in which the ideals of efficiency and profit erase the spheres of æsthetic emotion and realization of any oneness with Nature.

We may take Enclosure as both the best metaphor and the most rational implementation of such ideas. The spirit is closed off along with the Land. The poor will soon be declared "unfit", and they are already seen as undeserving. What counts is what is countable. The supposedly positive ideals of Rationalism, such as representative democracy, are at once betrayed by the "return of the repressed" and transmogrified into curses such as industrial Capitalism — and Terror.

Compared to this, Sumer and Egypt and the chivalry of King Arthur look actually attractive. Compared to Imperialist Colonialism and the Satanic mills of the Industrial Revolution, even medieval Christianity acquires a retrospective nostalgic glow — hence the "reactionary" aspect of Romanticism. But this reaction appears warm and revolutionary in contrast with the heartlessness and frigidity of Pure Reason. Moreover, there exists a "left wing" of Romanticism as well, exemplified by Shelley's and Byron's support for the Luddite weavers, and Blake's enthusiasm for Satan (in *The Marriage of Heaven and Hell*) as the Imagination. In response to rationalism naturally the free spirit may embrace the irrational — and the revolt of submerged consciousness will take on such "mad" forms as the Occult Revival of the 18th century, or the Decadence of the 19th, or Surrealism and Anarchism of the 20th. What we have called normal consciousness (as exemplified by Paleolithic culture) is now consigned to Bedlam. Only the insane are truly conscious.

---

4 See *Green Hermeticism: Alchemy and Ecology*, Christopher Bamford, Kevin Townley, & Peter Lamborn Wilson (2007).
5 Newton himself was split between his alchemical Christian self and his materialist rationalist self — "last of the Sumerians" and first of the moderns as Lord Keynes put it.

8. Bourgeois Self-Consciousness.

Now we arrive at what might be called the modern *mentalité*. Education has now turned into a process of acculturation to the dogmas of rationalism and utilitarianism, and the result is the *over-educated self*, not the Renaissance polymath but the dissociated specialist. Sexual repression on a virtually industrial scale is required to create the discipline needed to survive and even thrive under Capitalism. But the result appears as a pathological level of acute self-awareness, the emergent dark shadow of the Rational Enlightened Ego. Nineteenth century thoughts cling to religion like a floating broken spar after a shipwreck, but where religion begins to fail, the bourgeois mind emerges in triumph. Social Darwinism perverts the whole idea of godless evolution into an excuse for eugenic repression of the working class and the "other races". Materialism erects hysterical rigid defenses against the sensual and the irrational. Official art degenerates into heavy kitsch and triumphalist bombast, while the mad Romantics are excluded as irrelevant or even evil (opium addicts! perverts! æsthetic criminals!).

Sick bourgeois consciousness regards itself regarding itself in the mirror of self. It cares for the self and cultivates it like an investment portfolio, but also fears it like an inner Mr. Hyde. Like a steam engine it derives its great energy from self-suppression. Wealth is now no longer a sign of divine election but of evolutionary perfection. It's morally good to be secretly miserable — it's the price of being advanced and civilized, a true Victorian lady or gentleman.

Meanwhile the "others" who have not reached this advanced stage, the poor, the "natives" and "savages" of the far-flung Empire's dark corners, represent the Unconscious. They must be oppressed even as the unconscious is suppressed and denied. They have remained at one with wild nature, and this fact makes them despicable and dispensable.

The valuable self is the bourgeois self. And in fact the poor, although *oppressed*, really appear less *repressed* than their masters. They are "childlike" — a term of abuse in the mouths of Rulers — but for the resistance perhaps a romantic truth. The poor have their pleasures: sex, drugs, unbridled festival and chaos. The poor may even possess a mystic awareness now lost to their more civilized betters. Or do I romanticize too much? The natives with their hopeless ghost dances, the peasants with their futile agrarian uprisings — are they somehow more in touch with "divine Nature" than the bourgeoisie? I say yes.

9. Hyper-bourgeois Self-consciousness and the discovery of the Unconscious.

Around 1900 the European Masters of the Universe "suddenly" realized they were brain-sick or soul-sick. They'd grown tired of sexual repression and self-sacrifice on the altars of Advanced Civilization. An odor of incipient revolt began to be sensed in the air of the last golden days of the long 19th century. Nietzsche and Freud discovered the Unconscious.[6] Perhaps one could get back in touch with the primal self, the Stone Age self so to speak, of undivided consciousness. Perhaps the key was psychotherapy. Or perhaps it was Art. Or both.

Unfortunately it was neither. The result of the eruption of the Unconscious was the apocalypse of total war — the short 20th century and the worst suffering humanity had (so far) ever experienced — a purge that almost extirpated the patient — an orgy of hate and murder. [7]

The Surrealists looked on the de-repression of the unconscious as a revolutionary act. But Freud had decided that in the end the unconscious had to be re-repressed (like a steam engine) in order to save Civilization from its discontents; what he failed to

---

6 I'm being facetious. The unconscious had always been known through visions, dreams, art, madness. But it had not yet been defined by a *logos* (as in "psychology"). Actually I prefer to use the term *sub*conscious, which implies that this "level" is accessible (via sub-mersion) whereas *un*conscious suggests a radical impenetrability. In this respect I always think of Salvador Dalí arriving in America in a deep-sea diver's suit, claiming he was going to plumb the depths of our national unconscious. He fainted from lack of air.

7 America was largely spared — which explains why "we" are so prosperous — and so morally clueless. Our deployment of the atomic bomb symbolizes this situation, which has not changed since 1945.

realize is that Civilization IS its discontents. Trying to put the lid back on the bubbling cauldron of the Id simply resulted in an explosion in which the ego nearly disintegrated (cultural "shell shock"). The trauma of the eruption has defined consciousness in our "post-war" period.[8]

In the 1950s Freudian and existentialist thought reached the level of popular "discourse". My generation grew up joking about each others' Oedipus Complexes and our neurotic angst. By the 1960s we were sick of being depressed and "beat" and decided to revolt against Civilization in the name of peace, joy, free sex, entheogenic hallucinogens, art and mystical realization. We were deadly serious about this "game" and severely disappointed when the Revolution of 1968 failed and was repressed by Capitalism (and Communism, its evil twin).

Oriental spirituality turned out not to be the final answer either — it simply added its influence to the emergence of a new hyper-bourgeois self-consciousness, smug in its righteous liberal politics and sentimental environmentalism. "Spirituality" now means you never have to say you're sorry for helping to fuck up the last remnants of the natural world. "Who, me? Why, I voted for Obama!" "I meditate!" "I eat local food and drive a hybrid car." "I give money to the Dalai Lama." "I demonstrated against the war." And so on.

The hyper-bourgeois self is the *precious self*. Nothing could be more precious than the bourgeois child, created in the image of the bourgeois family, the cynosure and quintessence of its smug self -satisfied exceptionalism. Poor children may still "go outside and play", perhaps unsupervised, maybe even bored — but the precious child is never released from the castle of devotion. Surrounded by hi-tech toys and computers, TVs and video games, shepherded from one "quality-time activity" to another, cooped up with other similar children of the same age in Social factories for the produc-

---

8 Post-war? Maybe the *era of permanent war* would better describe the period from 1945 till now. War now isn't so much the health of the State (as Randolph Bourne put it) as it is the prerequisite for the survival of Civilization "as we know it".

tion of de-socialized egos, the precious child's every whim is coddled, but only in the context of a stifling oedipal misery. The result is the spoiled ignorant self-centered consumer fetishist "adult" — the infantilized hyper-self-conscious isolated etiolated self of the post-modern "universal middle class".

Incidentally, do I exempt myself from this critique? I wish I could say I was a healthy-minded free-spirited working class Mr. Natural, but in fact like Nietzsche I'm only able to diagnose the miseries of "my class" because I'm part of it.

10. Flight from the Unconscious under Technopathocracy.

The unconscious proved to be a hideous burden — a nasty *thing* fit only to be shoved back under the sofa of civility along with the dustballs and roaches of a discredited Past.

Psychoanalysis and entheogenic/shamanic plants were felt to be too threatening, and were replaced with serotonin uptake inhibitors and tranquilizers. Who needs the unconscious when we've got Prozac and Ritalin? Children who show signs of revolt, or potential for future anti-social behaviors, can now be drugged into submission, cheaply and efficiently. For us efficiency is the excuse for *everything*. We'll destroy the world in the name of *convenience*. And moreover, we'll make a profit on it. (In fact we already have.)

The *screen* takes the place of the soul or *psyche*. The screen provides at last the "heaven of glass" once promised by the body-despising Gnostic Dualists. The screen provides us with all the ancient dreams of magic: far-seeing, future-seeing, instantaneity, telepathy, the universal Library of all Information all the time, maps that will prevent our ever being lost (or ever knowing where we are), all commodities, all desires (as long as they have a price — and what doesn't?) at the flick of a button — a Big Brother to watch over our every move and thought and protect us from Terrorists and sell us whatever we want even before we realize we want it — virtual immortality — virtual shamanic flight — virtual (ersatz) consciousness that's far more fun and less threatening than the consciousness we were born with — other peoples' bright new thoughts to replace our old tired ones — an instant link to our perpetual debt account (infinite credit) — a prosthetic soul. An alien intelligence in your pocket for $200. All on one tiny screen — our tiny magic *mirror*. (Are we not the fairest of them all?)

What does the pathetic meat brain and its repressed Paleolithic consciousness offer to compare to these riches? Who *needs* consciousness anyway? Why? What for?

Consciousness is merely the terminal node that receives the data of the Universal Screen. Otherwise it has no function that cannot be replaced by a pill. The machinic suppression of the unconscious leads, sure as shit, to the disappearance of consciousness as well. "Data" is better than God, better than the self, better than dreams, and it fulfills all our desires before we even conceive them.

The rule of sick machines — the Technopathocracy — allows us all to live as happy zombies, eaters of our own brains, consumers of our own false selves. Under the sign of Universal Value — money itself — the long sad history of consciousness falters to a whimpering conclusion. The world goes on — without us. Our simulacra, our android replacements, will henceforth live *for us*, leaving us to the peaceful nirvana of our smartphones and iPads. Instead of human society (which doesn't exist, as Baroness Thatcher told us) we will have our "social networks". Like the famous Boy in the Bubble we need never risk our immunity in a real world of nasty bug-ridden storm-wrecked Nature. We can "interact" forever with all the images we need to provide us with a world where the only idol is the empty self.

It's *too late* for consciousness. We have evolved beyond it. It's no longer a problem — the problem has been solved. The brain is a computer. The soul is a screen, a mirror — but the mirror is empty. Gone, gone, gone.

Celtomania

"green green I love you green"
— F. Garcia Lorca

When I was quite young, I found out I was part Irish and part Scottish — a combination about as common in America as flies on a windowscreen in August. However, it excited my imagination, and being a bookish child I at once began to feed myself on various forms of Celtic romanticism — King-Arthur-for-kids and whatnot. Somehow news about the IRA and the shenanigans of various Scottish secessionists filtered down into my consciousness, and I became a Celtic Nationalist.

I persuaded my pals to give up playing cowboys and Indians and instead (to their bewilderment) take up playing IRA vs Black & Tans. (The evil "Black and Tan" British auxiliaries had vanished from Ireland around 1921. But I didn't know that.)

I distinctly recollect learning with great satisfaction that some young rogue members of the Scottish National Party had broken into Westminster Abbey and stolen the Stone of Scone. This dull-looking rough-hewn boulder is connected by a very legendary legend with Tara, the seat of the High Kings of Ireland — but it was certainly used in the coronation of Scottish Kings for centuries, until the Brits stole it and put it under the Throne of England in Westminster, and used it in the coronation of their own monarchs up to and including Elizabeth II. The SNP refused to accept the re-stolen stone, so the young firebrands had to give it back. But in 1999, after the home-land achieved Home Rule, the English re-returned the stone to Scotland, although they said they intend to "borrow" it for further coronation ceremonies in London.

My maternal grandfather, Patrick "Pop" Rion (or Rian, or Ryan) hailed from an area of County Cork around Fermoy on the River Blackwater. In the middle ages it was said that the wicked gnostic magician Simon Magus (mentioned in *Acts of the Apostles*) had migrated to Fermoy. I'd like to claim him as an ancestor.

The Fermoy region enjoyed the honor of appointing all the Chief Druids of the King of Munster (the South "quarter" of Ireland) at the Rock of Cashel. Great grandfather was a "Gaelic Protestant", i.e., a convert from Catholicism to the Anglican Church of Ireland. For many years he drove electric trolley cars from Baltimore to Washington D.C.; as the old ballad said, he'd come to America "to work upon the railway" like thousands of other Irish emigrants.

I presume the Wilsons (of Georgetown D.C.) were Scots of the large and amorphous Wilson clan, but I've heard a family rumor of Welsh origin. I can't trace the genealogy back to Europe. It would be nice to claim some Welsh blood as well as Irish and Scottish. In any case the really interesting Scots connection came through my father's mother, who was a Cranston.

The second and third governors of colonial Rhode Island were Cranstons and the elder married a daughter of the first governor, Roger Williams. One of the two was accused of secret dealings with pirates and is often remembered for hanging thirteen pirates at one shot. In Scotland the Cranstons were themselves known as "Border Reivers", i.e., land pirates. Their family motto reads, "Thou shalt want ere I want" — a good slogan for kleptomaniacs, to be sure. (The coat of arms was a "canting" or punning image of a *Crane* with a *stone* in its claw. The badge was a strawberry.)

One of the 16th century Cranston lairds married Elizabeth Stuart, god-daughter and namesake of Queen Elizabeth I and daughter of Francis Stewart, Fifth Earl of Bothwell, who was first cousin to King James VI/I and favorite nephew of Mary Queen of Scots.

I plan to write a whole essay on Earl Francis, but here I'll just mention that he is best remembered for attempting, on Halloween 1590, to assassinate his cousin King James by witchcraft. Apparently he considered that he himself had a good claim to the Throne, and since he'd studied magic in Italy, and knew at least seventy witches, he convened a coven of them in North Berwick to put a spell on James's ship and sink it by a storm. The spell failed and Bothwell ended up fleeing back to Italy, where he continued (according to Montague Summers) to practice "necromancy" in Naples till he died — amazingly, not by violence.

Naturally I was not only a supporter of the IRA and SNP, I also became a Jacobite, an advocate of the right of the Stuart family to the Throne of Scotland, Ireland, England and France. I admired the Cavaliers, not the Roundheads (I still hate Puritans) or the Hanoverians. Later in England in the 1970s, I met a few doddering old Jacobites, but by now (2014) there seem to be none left. The Northumbrian Jacobite Society, which I also recently joined, seems more interested in re-enactments than revenge for Culloden. I've corresponded with one Count Peter Pininski of Poland, who *could* be the Pretender if he wanted to proclaim himself, but has merely contented himself with writing a book explaining how he is descended from Bonnie Prince Charlie — directly but illegitimately. He has no royal ambitions, unfortunately.

In my high school freshman year history course I wrote a research paper on the Cranstons and got an A-plus. Around this same time I was discovering anarchism and beginning to consider myself an anarchist. As I've explained in *Heresies*, my "anarchist memoirs", I was never able to renounce Celtic Nationalism and Jacobitism even after embracing "libertarian socialism" and anti-authoritarian Individualism. For years I tended to drift back and forth between these "lost causes", but finally in 1980 (in Rome, as it happened) I suddenly realized that anarchy and monarchy are both the *politics of dream* ("oneirocracy") and I decided to amalgamate them and believe in "two impossible things" at once, to paraphrase *Alice*. Sometimes I call myself an ambulatory schizophrenic, sometimes I call myself an anarcho-monarchist. I discovered that the brilliant Populist demagogue Governor Huey P. Long of Louisiana coined the slogan "Every Man a King — But no-one wears the Crown." Change that to "every *person* a *monarch*" — and take it literally — and it would sum up my position nicely. Do I contradict myself? Heck, my father was editor-in-chief of the Harvard *Complete Works* of Emerson — why should I worry about "consistency—the hobgoblin of little minds"?

In the 1980s some anarchists used the term "champagne revolution", meaning that everyone should enjoy the pleasures of the rich. "If I can't dance I don't want your revolution", as Emma Goldman put it. "Every man and every woman is a star", as the wicked Magus Aleister Crowley said (in *Liber legis*).

Can I explain how this ideal could be achieved in practice? Yes, and it's not too difficult. It already existed in the remote past, before the emergence of the State, when every human was free and sovereign, within the context of Mutual Aid (i.e., the "tribe"). And it very nearly existed in the 1970s in Scandinavia and Holland. Those countries with monarchs who "reigned without ruling" inaugurated radical Social Democratic regimes that we can admit were as good as the State has ever been: welfare and healthcare for all, 90% income tax on the rich, total support for the arts, sexual freedom, environmental consciousness, etc. Best of all, under such lax control, anarchist alternatives proved to be both feasible and popular. Think of the scene in Amsterdam in the '70s — the "Gnome Party" won seats on the City Council, white bicycles were available for free, pot was de-criminalized, squats blossomed, people lived without money. Of course all this came to a sad end when Reagan and Thatcher took over the universe — but Monarcho-Socialism was great while it lasted. Why shouldn't it come back again? (Unless we're all simply doomed.)

I believe that if Scotland is ever to become a real republic, like Eire, it should offer the throne of the country to a Stuart. Maybe to Count Pininski. The SNP should then join with Scottish Labour to institute radical Social Democracy, Scandinavian style, and begin to lead the world out of the Slough of Capitalist Despond. Meanwhile I'll emigrate to Scotland and help inaugurate a loyal anarchist opposition devoted to *real* non-authoritarian alternatives like producers' co-ops, free schools, free-love communes — and neo-pagan revivalism. Eventually the State would "wither away" and utopia would be attained.

O well, it's a nice thought.

I joined the Celtic League in the early '90s when it was still more-or-less being run by Alexei Kondratiev, amazing Celtic philologist and gay neo-druid (he wrote a nice little book on Celtic Mysteries). He died too young, but in his memory I still keep up my subscription to the journal. One high point of my membership was meeting the League's leaders (including B. Moffett of the Isle of Man) at a bizarre "Philosophy" conference I attended in Libya during the Qadaffi era, where every lost cause in the world was represented, from the Turkish Green Party to French Maoists,

French "New Rightist", Alain de Benoist, a Slovenian anarchist, a few old African socialists . . . an ideological circus.

The goals of the League include independence for the six major unfree Celtic nations: Wales, Scotland, Cornwall, Man, Brittany and Northern Ireland. Language activism plays an even bigger role however. While I fully agree that all languages (including "Native American" and other "Fourth World" tongues) should not just survive but thrive, I'm afraid I've been too lazy to learn Irish or Welsh, which I'd've chosen for their great literatures. But I'd make an argument (against the League's stated philosophy) that other languages have become "Celtic" by adoption, including Gallego (spoken in Galician Spain and Portugal by enthusiastic Celts) — and English, a major language, after all, of the Celtic Revival or "Twilight". W.B. Yeats and Hugh MacDiarmid wrote in English; I rest my case. I also take an interest in Galatia, the Celtic part of Turkey (including Ankara and Konya), where Gaulish was spoken from circa 300 B.C—500 A.D., and St Paul famously scolded the Celts for their laxity and heresy. Celtic words seem to have entered the Turkish language, according to at least one "mad" philologist, and I dare say that DNA testing would turn up plenty of Turkish Celtic genes. I suspect that certain Turkish Sufi heretics, such as the Bektashis (who drink wine) may preserve ancient druidic "mysteries".

Any anarchist, like any "socialist", can support the cause of secession and independence for colonized peoples, on the assumption that anarchism (or communism or whatever) would be too difficult to attain under conditions of actual oppression. James Connolly believed this about Ireland, and died for the Cause in 1916. Anyway, that is my excuse for my own hopeless 19th century Romanticism and Celtomania.

By the way, the Atlantic Celts are certainly not a "pure Indo-European race". Far more "blood" belongs to original Cro-Magnon (or even Neanderthal) ancestry than to Indo-Europeans. (I say this in part on the basis of actual DNA-test population genetics, although I don't necessarily believe that this science has attained infallibility.) Celtic culture is a mix of "Old Europe" and Indo-European; only the languages are *perhaps* "pure", although some Celtic scholars believe in a pre-IE structural "substratum", not to mention possible pre-IE place names. (On this see one of my favorite books, *Atlantean: Ireland's North African and Maritime Heritage* by old friend Bob Quinn.) Celticism is not "racism"! You might ask, if it's also not strictly a matter of language, then what is it? I'd say that for me it's a "mystery", a spirit, a tincture of life and culture that fascinates me. Alexei was a Russian, and he was the most enthusiastic Celtophile I've ever known. "Family" should be considered significant (ask any anthropologist) — but it's not everything — not by a long shot. "My heart's in the Highlands", and that's that.

Actually my heart is more in Midlothian, Walter Scott country, between Edinburgh and the Border, where the Cranstons live. (The Cranstons appear in Scott's first best-selling poem, "Lay of the Last Minstrel", where they are depicted as involved in witchcraft and haunted by a "goblin butler").

My first trip to Ireland, in 1991, was paid for by Gordon Campbell, a selfmade millionaire who'd organized a Brion Gysin festival in Dublin and wanted me to speak there. All sorts of old Gysin/Burroughs characters showed up including the Jajouka Master Musicians of Morocco, and events were held in various storefronts in Temple Bar (which later became a very chic neighborhood) and Gordon's abandoned candy factory in Castle St. (which later became his penthouse and short-lived radical bookstore, Garden of Delight — G.O.D. for short).

I loved Dublin, especially the sad decaying Georgian neighborhoods, and Bewley's Oriental Tea Shop in Grafton St., where every day Gordon's friend the Joyce scholar and spoiled monk Patrick Healey held forth at a table of seedy queer brilliant artists and scholars, over tea and black puddings. I loved the National Library with its Georgian dome and sky-lights over the Reading Room where I had my own desk and "worked" many happy days on Irish folklore, breaking for lunch at the National Museum across the way, and high tea at the famous old Shelbourne Hotel nearby on St Stephen's Green. Gordon introduced me to dozens of fascinating people, including Gareth Brown, founder of Claddagh Records, who owned a vast exquisite estate in the Wicklow

Mountains outside Dublin, called Luggala, where Brendan Behan (queer anarchist genius) and many other artistic luminaries had once overindulged in Gareth's liquor cabinet. Booze is the seductive plague of Ireland. I've never drunk so much. Guinness every day in the pub, wine every meal except breakfast. "Whiskey" is an Irish word meaning "water". Gareth had his own family uilann piper, Ronan Brown, a great musician. He and Gareth helped me with my collection of Irish music revealed by the Fairies, which I later played on WBAI-FM in New York City, on my show, "The Moorish Orthodox Radio Crusade".

The G.O.D. only lasted about two years but this constituted a little golden age for me and Gordon (though he lost a lot of money) and our brilliant managers Jake Rabinowitz and the radical troublemaker Alan Toner. We hung out drinking coffee with Dublin's finest leftist poets and freeloaders, including our friend the American artist James Mathers, a descendant of S.L. MacGregor Mathers of the Golden Dawn. The whole staff pitched in to help publish my political essays written in or about Ireland, *Millennium* (co-published with Autonomedia of Brooklyn). We founded the Holy Order of the Lemon to rag the Protestant Orange Order, and organized a march of about 100 people all dressed in black derby hats and yellow ribbons, to throw lemons into the River Liffey — we made the newspapers (and also Robert Anton Wilson's last book, *Everything's Under Control*). We also held readings and art shows and parties.

In Dublin I always stayed in Gordon's house (Georgian of course) in an old suburb, and we also went often to his summer house, a totally crazy erection of stone and glass designed by Gordon himself and built on a hilltop overlooking Ballinskellig in County Kerry. This little village is the taking-off port for Skellig Michael, a sugarloaf rock in the sea once inhabited by Celtic monks. The local pub was run by more spoiled monks and was the hang-out of the stoned shannachie (Irish tradition-holder) Mick Murphy, whom I wrote about in my poetry collection *Ec(o)logues*, along with other Irish subjects. We also spent time in County Cork in a castle called Saffron (part Norman part Georgian), where friends of Gordon's were cultivating culinary mushrooms. They also supplied us with magic fungi for our greatest stunt, a Midsummer Night's party for about 60 people at an undisclosed outdoor location near Newgrange and Knowth, where amazingly no one failed to have a great time, and several experienced Faery visions.

Not all our time was spent partying. I conceived a great interest in Megaliths (pre-Celtic) and Iron Age stone structures (Celtic). We started with Newgrange — overrun with tourists and badly restored (it looks like a Neolithic car-park) but still very impressive. We failed to get into Dowth, the (privately owned) "Halloween" Megalith, and were chased away by an angry farmer. But we wrangled a special invitation to enter Knowth, still being dug up by archæologists, on a Sunday when we had the huge corbel -vaulted central "cathedral" to ourselves, smoked hash and communed with the spirits.

Another great trip with Gordon, out to Co Leitrim and Sligo in the West, was devoted to visiting the battlefield of Moytura, where the Tuatha De Danaan (i.e., the Faeries) fought against the Fomorians, the "Giants". My researches in the National Library were largely devoted to the Fomorians, who I believe were the original Cro-Magnon/Neanderthal inhabitants of Ireland, and who were struggling against the invading Celts, (the Faeries being the Celtic gods). I've written about them in my *Ploughing The Clouds: The Search for Irish Soma* (City Lights).

We were rooming with a nice lady who happened to be a witch, and lived between the two "fairy forts" made famous by a piece of music transcribed by the 17th century blind harper Turlough O'Carolan (the most beautiful of all tunes ever given to a human by the Fairies). She tried to help us find the megalithic tomb of Nuala Silverhand, the leader of the Tuatha De at Moytura, which she'd "never been able to locate". By sheer "chance" we nearly ran into a car, on a narrow boreen, which turned out to belong to the farmer who actually owned the tomb, who gladly took us to see it, in an obscure field behind his house, in "soft" rain — a very Irish moment.

Which reminds me of the day I spent roaming around Wicklow with the piper Ronan Brown from pub to pub, listening to fairy music on the tape machine in his car, when he decided to look for a stone circle he'd "never been able to find". As we were crashing through the woods in the rain near where it ought to have been we happened suddenly to notice a "fairy ring" of magic mushrooms, the little ones called "pookies" (named after a kind of fairy) — and when we looked up — there was the stone circle. This kind of thing happens in Ireland *all the time* — once you start searching for it, anyway. In that respect it reminded me very much of India.

Gordon organized another art event: a re-creation of Joseph Beuys's "7000 Oaks" — a planting of trees along with "magic" stone plinths, which Beuys originally carried out in Cassel, Germany, and urged people all over the world to emulate. Gordon found a farmer in Uisnach to take the saplings, and he obtained the baby trees somehow. Uisnach is the ancient ceremonial "navel" of Ireland, where the omphalos stone that marks the Center of the land is still to be seen, along with some megalithic ruins, in the middle of a muddy cow pasture. My friend the Beuys scholar David Levi Strauss and I flew over from America to attend the event. About fifty people came and each one got to plant a tree (in the rain of course) — we then retired to a nearby Georgian mansion and drank champagne.

Levi and I later went on a pilgrimage to see the Charleville Oak, the 600-year-old druidic tree which had supplied the acorns for Uisnach, and arrived in front of the magisterial huge entity on Halloween afternoon. Two witches were sacrificing to the spirit there.

We then drove on to Northern Ireland to see an art gallery in Derry. The owner took us to visit the Grianan of Aileach (the "sun fort"), an Iron Age stone castle on a hilltop outside the City. The fort is associated with the Dagda, the "good god" of the Celts, whom I had actually seen in a mushroom vision. While we were there the rain paused for a moment and the biggest brightest rainbow I've ever experienced appeared with one end touching the fort and the other far off across the valley. We felt we could walk on it, and find the treasure buried at its foot.

I don't want to turn this into yet another whole book about exotic Ireland, so I'll just briefly recall our trip (along with Gordon's pal John Stevenson, the young politician and ne'er-do-well) to Aran Island, on Beltane (May Day), to take part in a ritual bonfire with some charming Catholic anarchists; and our pilgrimage to the Temple of Isis in Waterford, the most dilapidated castle I've ever seen that was actually still inhabited, where scenes of the film "Barry Lyndon" were shot; and the second-most dilapidated castle, complete with rusting suits of armor and cobwebs, owned by a Guinness heiress and art patroness who kept a bevy of ragged geniuses in her Georgian stables. You can't make this shit up.

I must devote a paragraph to Irish food, which is surprisingly great. Here are some of the memorable meals I ate there: Galway oysters with brown bread and butter and Murphy's Stout (Irish bread is wonderful, unlike English bread). Fresh turbot, rack of local spring lamb with new potatoes, and claret, in Waterville, County Derry. Whole poached wild salmon — many times. Full Irish breakfast at Bewley's: fried eggs, sausage, ham, bacon, fried tomatoes, fried mushroom, black pudding, white pudding, fried toast and pots and pots of tea. ("Irish" tea is actually from Assam, India, a place I once visited to make a pilgrimage to the Vagina of the Goddess.) Nettle soup in County Cork (fresh spring nettles in chicken broth and cream — try it!) along with lots of mushrooms grown by our friends at Castle Saffron, served in omelets, on pasta, or with roast beef — and *plenty* of red wine, followed by Power's whiskey and pookies. Cushlamachree! Boiled whole farm bacon with white parsley sauce (Gordon's recipe) — and wine. Wild strawberries with *real* whipped cream (no reddiwhip in Ireland!) at the cafeteria in the National Museum in Dublin (where Gordon and I went to see the secret collection of Sheila-na-gigs — speaking of Goddess's vaginas — long before they were shown openly to the public). Some of these places didn't come cheap, but I must admit this was one of the advantages of having a friend and patron who was a millionaire. Gordon sadly died far too young, and I miss him terribly. Thanks to him and his "Academy of Everything is Possible" I enjoyed some of the best days (and meals) of my life. I dedicate this essay to his memory.

Before quitting Ireland let me say that above all it was the land itself that made the deepest impression on me, so much so that I felt déjà vu—haunted wherever I went, as if remembering a prior incarnation. I seemed to be *at home* there from the first day I landed in Dublin (what other airport in the world could have boasted a *poetry shop?*). Ireland is underpopulated (more sheep and cows than humans) and much of it consists of just landscape, punctuated by ruined Norman towers and fairy hills overgrown with blackthorn. And the color green in Ireland is *more green* than anywhere else in the world — honest. John Stevenson once coddled me into believing that vast amounts of copper in the soil produce the saturated spectrum of greens. Maybe it's even true — or maybe it's just the incessant beautiful rain drifting down like a continual blessing, and the Celtic mist. I once saw moss growing *inside* a Dublin omnibus.

Leaving aside Ireland's "tragic history" of oppression, violence and religious bigotry — both Catholic and Protestant — and going back to the Romano-Celtic era from about 100 to 600 A.D. — the Ireland remembered in the medieval romances — it is fascinating to note that the early Celtic Christian Church in Ireland had *no martyrs*. Not one saint was ever killed by Irish pagans. Somehow the druidic faith seems to have been absorbed into the new religion in some kind of voodoo-like syncresis — now long lost, but devoutly desired by modern neo-Celtic enthusiasts. St Columba, for instance, who protected and patronized the "pagan" Order of Bards, is quoted as having proclaimed that "Christ is my Druid".

Later on when Catholic Rome finally "invaded" the Celtic lands, this ur-Church was suppressed — then the Vikings descended like a plague — then the Normans — then the Elizabethans — Cromwell — and so on and so on. And yet beneath all that there still persisted a living underground magical tradition that came to light again in the Celtic Revival of the 19th century, and a paganochristian poetry of life that I — along with millions of other romantics — find irresistible. It's slightly *sad*, no doubt heavily suffused with *Twilight* — but still authentic, wholly itself, non-ironic, complex but pure.

Ronan Brown once told us about an old custom in North Dublin (the poor side of the River): on Sundays by law the pubs had to close from noon to 4 pm — but certain pubs simply locked the doors and everyone stayed inside all afternoon having a *ceili*, i.e., a party devoted to music, poetry and booze. "Now", he said, "the law is about to be changed and relaxed, and pubs will be allowed to stay open Sunday afternoons. The lock-in tradition will come to an end. I know one pub which is going to have one last blow-out this sabbath before the law changes. Come with me."

So we did — with a gaggle of families complete with kids and dogs — and spent four happy hours listening to traditional music and folk poetry, including one long ridiculous comic ballad about a drunken "donnybrook" or senseless brawl, and we drank Guinness after Guinness till we stumbled out into the melancholy evening.

Appendix: Fairy Music

Unfortunately I made my collection of Irish Fairy music some 20 years ago, and since then have lost both the recordings and the playlist. I remember that my goal (other than sheer fun) was to discover if any difference could be detected between music "learned from the Fairies" and the general body of Irish music. I suppose I expected to find the Tuatha De Danaan preferred slow airs in minor keys or something. In fact, however, they turned out to like all sorts of music and song, from slow airs in minor keys to the most cheerful fast jigs. It seems their taste was simply for Irish music, but only the best. In any case one of the big themes of the folklore (or direct first-person narrative) about hearing fairy music is that it vastly improves the playing of the human who undergoes the initiation. A common story concerns the amateur musician who has "only two tunes" but meets a "wee red-haired man" who caresses the man's fiddle three times, after which he can play everything in the repertoire with supernatural technique (e.g., rich ornamentation etc.). The great 18th century blind harper Carolan was considered to be a useless idiot till he heard the Fairies playing, after which he became a great composer and performer. A number of musicians who actually recorded their work claimed to have had this experience.

Among those "touched" musicians who recorded were the great fiddlers Néillidh Boyle and Junior Crehan. Other younger players have learned directly from such older initiated performers.

The good news is that a number of these artists are featured on a 2-CD set recently released with a book of commentary, entitled *The Otherworld: Music and Song from Irish Tradition,* ed. by R. uí Ógáin and T. Sherlock (Comhairle Bhéalvideas Èireann, Dublin, 2012). (It can be ordered for $40 from Four Courts Press c/o International Specialized Book services, 920 NE 58th Ave Suite 300, Portland Oregon 97213-3786; tel. 1-800-944-6190, or fcp@isbs.com.)

This splendid collection is mostly based on recordings made by field-workers of the great National Folklore Collection (now part of the University of Dublin), a vast and still largely-untapped hoard of texts and tapes dating back to the 1930s. I visited the NFC while carrying out my project — but the editors of *The Other World* have been working hard there for 20 years, and their collection is far more authentic and wide-raging than mine, based as it was only on commercial recordings.

Another difference between my project and *The Otherworld* is that mine dealt only with music "learned from the Fairies", while the new collection covers all aspects of the relations amongst narrative and music and the supernatural in general. Songs about ghosts and banshees are included, for instance, without necessarily being *by* or *from* these entities. All the Irish songs are nicely translated and reveal (as so often) a brilliant poetic sensibility which seems somehow "typically Celtic" — especially in the *sean-nos* songs, unaccompanied and devilishly complex, using metres based on wild runs of verbal ornamentation — within strange "oriental"-sounding pentatonic melodies. Part of the "magic" of certain Irish music in general, fairies or no fairies, is its ability to evoke tears without using cheap sentimentality — while the fast jigs and hornpipes evoke *hilaritas* without cheap vulgarity. This collection, I repeat, is as *authentic* as can be, and therefore deeply moving, whether to gloom or cheer.

If it seems impossible to distinguish stylistically between fairy music and "merely human" music in the Irish tradition, perhaps this confusion arises from that tradition's liminal condition, floating between the two ontological planes and thus creating an æsthetic that reflects *as a whole* a mingling of this world with the otherworld. All Irish music, in this sense, can be seen as initiatic.

Although no doubt Ireland has its share of "normal" prosaic souls, somehow I seemed to meet there with an unusual number of pixilated "touched" inspired and eccentric fellow humans. The word "mad" is used in Ireland as a term of endearment and praise; it doesn't mean "insane" but rather enlarged by *the afflatus of genius,* and therefore more than merely normal. I apologize if this seems an "essentialist" cliché touted by a "helpless romantic", but I have to call things as I saw them. I've always been amazed, as I travelled around the world, at how often cultural stereotypes emerge to trump our modern liberal desire to believe that everyone is "equal" in a flat universe of "democratic" indifference. The truth I prefer to see is that difference is real and makes life interesting. And as my distant cousin and friend the late wit and Celtophile Robert Anton Wilson used to say, an Irish fact has a special flavor or (if you insist) essence that transcends the quotidian dullness of the merely actual. The Irish stereotype of lyrical, eloquent, "twi-lit" and slightly supernatural or fey charm and brilliance just happens to be real — or as real as it needs to be.

The great Irish composer Sean O'Riada detected a secret and direct link between Irish and Indian music, or Indo-European culture in general. It involves a kind of permeability between the spheres of "the gods" (or fairies) and humans, as if the wall that separates them were thinner in India and Ireland than elsewhere. In this sense writers like AE or Lord Dunsany are merely realists: they see through the wall and describe what they see. Similarly, from druid times to Carolan's 18th century , to the Celtic magical revival of the mid-20th century, Irish musicians play what they hear from "over there".

In my experience it was impossible to go ten miles in Ireland without falling under some spell. Even the weather seemed enchanting — literally — since the "soft" rain and mist turned any cow pasture or ruined barn into a bit of fairy landscape — not to mention the holy wells, megaliths, medieval round towers or decaying Georgian mansions. If a certain melancholy comes with this package, so to speak, surely it is better to be slightly haunted than merely human.

Against Celtoscepticism

Since I try to keep up with Celtic studies I can tell you that the latest fashionable theory in the field is called *Celtoscepticism*, and consists (in a nutshell) of the contention that Celts don't exist — that "Celtic" is a 19th century pseudo-category — that there is no Celtic "origin" (in fact *origins* in general do not exist) — and no Celtic "essence". To believe in essence is pseudo-nationalistic and fascistic. [1]

Now, just for laughs I'd like to see one of these self-proclaimed Celtosceptics walk up to a Black person and say Black people don't exist, that the notion was invented in the 19th century by white abolitionists, that the "Africa" origin-myth is a pseudo-construct, etc. Or go face-to-face with an "American Indian" and explain that the term means "a person from India named for an Italian conquistador", and that "you people" only arrived in America in 15,000 BC and are thus no more "indigenous" than we Europeans. Go ahead, try it!

And just as an aside: all the Celtosceptics I've noticed so far seem to have German or English names. Could it be that this new post-post-deconstructionist academic bullshit merely masks the same dreary old Empire-chauvinistic disdain for inferior types who claim England has been colonizing them and fucking them over for centuries, and that it's time to secede and reclaim their freedom? Remember it wasn't long ago that *Punch* magazine depicted all Irishmen as stupid apes. There's *essentialism* for you! OK, now they're not simian morons — they just *don't exist!*

---

1 See for example Raimund Karl, "The Celts from Everywhere and Nowhere", in *Celtic from the West: Alternative Perspectives from Archæology, Genetics, Language, and Literature*, ed. B Cunliffe and J.T. Koch (Oxford, 2012). Note that Karl's is the only Celtosceptic essay in an otherwise excellent collection of papers, most of which explore the possibility that Celtic languages may first have arisen in Megalithic Iberia. A fascinating corollary of this idea is that the old Irish *Book of Invasions*, which posits a "Spanish" origin for the "Milesian Gaels", may no longer be considered a gallimaufry of late medieval fake-lore. It's now possible to argue that the myth contains some truth. See esp. Koch's essay on Tartessian as a Celtic language.

Naturally I admit that the famous "identity politics of the 1970s" raised vexing problems and contradictions that remain still unresolved. Nevertheless I object to throwing the babies of identity out with the bathwater of false consciousness in the name of a spurious and specious humanistic homogeneity that exists only in feel-good propaganda images concocted by wishy-washy liberal academics.

Underlying such ideas as the denial of identity I find the unspoken supposition that "we" — bourgeois mostly-white Euro-Americans — constitute the NORM of humanity. *We* have no "identity" because we represent evolutionary perfection. *We* are not "different"— *they* are different. The Others. But if only they would wake up and join our Real Civilization, they too would no longer have an "identity" other than — bourgeois Euro-American college graduates with progressive liberal attitudes and no detectable regional accents.

Many "Leftists" either deny that "identity" exists at all, or else they claim to be "race Traitors" to the (lower-case) "white" race, which of course doesn't exist. (God forbid anyone should claim to be *Indo-European*!) Jews are (grudgingly) allowed to be Jews, but the goyim are simply nothing — because "we" are the role model for all real people — and real people are nothing. We have no "origin" — no beginning — and no end, no "destiny".

"Full disclosure", as the current cliché has it: — I am a (mongrel) Celt; that is, I have a mix of Irish, Scotch-Irish, Scots, Welsh, Breton, Saxon, Norman, African and American Indian ancestors, and I "identify" culturally as a Celt, not as a Bourgeois Nothing-Person. I don't speak a Celtic language, but I have heard it done, and have wondered how people who speak "Celtic" could possibly not exist.

One reason for my claim arises from my membership in the Moorish Orthodox Church of America, a psychedelic religion of the 1960s, an offshoot of the Moorish Science Temple of America, which was founded by a Prophet of mixed Moorish and Cherokee heritage, Noble Drew Ali, in Newark New Jersey in 1913. He claimed that Celts are an "Asiatic Race" and therefore eligible to play a part in the *Moorish Empire*;[2] other European-Americans who joined the movement he called "Persians" — and I lived in Persia for seven years, so I'm "part Persian" (at least molecularly).[3]

It should go without saying that my Celtomania does not extend to kitsch manifestations of cultural leprechaunism or political revanchism, racism of any sort, or sentimental touristic pseudo-heritage worship. However, I confess to an emotional attachment (since childhood) to the cause of Celtic freedom from perfidious Albion (an independent Ireland, Scotland, Wales, Cornwall and Isle of Man) and from Imperial France (Brittany), just as I support freedom for Catalonia, Basque-land, and even Celtic Galicia, and Western Sahara, and the Republic of Vermont. As an anarchist, I believe, like Lysander Spooner, that every region should secede from every State, and that every human should secede from every authoritarian social structure. Proudhonian Mutualism would constitute the ideal — a federation of free communes and individuals. Thus I support first independence for Scotland, then democratic socialism, then anarchism — step by step. I support the Celtic language movement — I see no reason why English should triumph *über alles* in the form of bad internet prose. I support Celtic music, poetry, art and even costume. I love *difference* as long as it's free of hegemony and oppression. I hate sameness, conformity, global Capitalism and its mediated Konsumer Kultur. As a luddite I favor atavisms and reversions. Progress sucks, basically.

---

2 Asiatic branches of the Celts include the Scythians (according to the *Book of Invasions*) and of course the Galatians, who conquered Central Anatolia in the third century BC and were still speaking "Celtic" when St Paul wrote them his famous *Letter*. One can find Celtic words in modern Turkish. The Tocharians (Yueh-Chi, or Kushans) lived in Western China during the Han Dynasty and later conquered Balkh and North India, spoke an I-E tongue more closely related to Celtic than to Indo-Iranian, and wore woolen cloths like Scottish tartans. See *The Mummies of Urumchi*, J. Mallory, *et al.*

3 Evans-Wentz hypothesized a direct link between *"Iran"* and *"Eirenn"* or Ireland — both terms related to *Aryan*, or "noble". This may or may not be literally true, but it's interesting.

So much for subjectivity.

Philosophically (or "objectively") there remains much to say about *origins* and *essences*. Briefly, then, I propose a critique of post-Marxist post-post-Deconstruction and its dismissal of all originary thought. In the 19th century various savants proposed various origins for "religion" (i.e., for structured metaphysical cognition), such as Vegetation, Fertility, Solar cult, stone-worship, snake-worship, and so on. Each of these notions was typically proposed as the sole exclusive origin of human philosophical thought. Obviously, to us now all of them were bogus — if taken as the One True Explanation of Everything. We are all "relativists" now. But does it follow therefore that these systems were totally devoid of interest or of "relative" truth? Why should we assume that these babies are polluted irreparably by their bathwater? Each of them has its good points. All life is sacred. Frazer's obsession with fertility doesn't render *The Golden Bough* useless or empty of truths. Obviously "fertility" is AN origin of the human social — how could it not be? And Macrobius's obsession with Solar cults, later taken up by various Victorian scholars, holds great interest. Why shouldn't it?

The same argument holds true, *mutatis mutandis*, for all theories of human sodality, of the "Social" itself. On various levels we can speak of kinship, co-evolutionary mutualism, economic advantage, spirituality, innate simian band-instinct, language, cooperative hunting/gathering and so on and so forth, as "origins of the Social". To privilege any single origin leads to contradictions. But to accept ALL origins might lead to a kind of truth. I propose a palimpsestic overlayering and syncresis of all origins — in fact, a *delirium of origins*.

The problem with Structuralism lay in its dyadic or (let's be frank) dualistic view of the social. "Raw and cooked" doesn't begin to exhaust the complexities of the social as "cuisine", for example. It's an interesting epistemological device, and should not be discarded. But it needs to be vastly expanded. Post-structuralism reduced the "Two" to "Zero": no origin , no essence. I'd prefer to enlarge it to infinity: endless ramifications, with pathways negotiating the complexity. "From the one (the *Tao*) arose the two (*Yin & Yang*); from the two arose the 10,000 things." The *I Ching*, with its

64 hexagrams and their variations give a power structure with virtually innumerable originary movements; this begins to sound like a usable sociology. We have suffered too long under vulgar Cartesian either/or reductionism — our greatest triumph, the computer, has only two modes of "thought" — on and off. What conceptual poverty!

Gustav Landauer, the most important anarchist thinker of the 20th century, a Jewish Nietzschean, martyred by proto-fascist thugs in 1919, propounded a view of social freedom that is now almost totally forgotten. For him, as for us, the concept of biological race could only be seen as an empty illusion. But he embraced the idea of the *volk,* the people, the positive valuation of difference among cultural heritages. All volks are of course "equal" and there can be no question of hegemonic hierarchy. Each volk has its own genius, in the Latin sense, if you like, or presiding angel.[4]

This leftwing volkism does not rule out cosmopolitan complexity or, for that matter, a Nietzschean mingling of heritages. After all, we are all mongrels of some sort, if only thanks to our 4% Neanderthal genetic heritage. But there also exists what we might call a *pleasure of the volk,* which ought to be seen as something to treasure rather than despise. Sadly, the whole concept of the volk was to be highjacked, perverted and ruined, by the ideological monsters of the 20th century, and now seems to survive only as hateful chauvinism and xenophobia. But once there existed a positive socialist humanism of the volk. It could have meaning again for us.

Since the collapse of the Historical Movement of the Social in 1989-91, we have lived in a "global" world where Capitalism claims triumphantly to exist as the sole super-ideology. In response to this hegemony, since "socialism" no longer seems viable, there has risen a plethora of sub-ideological *reactions* to Kapital. Among

---

4 Walter Benjamin and Gersholm Scholem were influenced in their student days by this idea, via Martin Buber — see his *Pathways in Utopia.* There then existed a movement of anarcho-Zionism, a Jewish branch of the left/anarchist German Youth movement, the Jung Wandervogel, etc. See W. Laquer's *The German Youth Movement,* still the only English-language historical study of this fascinating lost era.

them, nationalism, racism, xenophobia, religious fundamentalism, and other post-fascistic tendencies. One can sympathize with peoples' hatred of "the American way", or "Europeanism" without wishing to share their sickness. Surely a *social* alternative must exist.

And in fact not all "separatist" movements can be dismissed as reactionary. The Kurdish insurgents in the three autonomist Syrian provinces are the last real secular leftists on the ground in the whole Middle East — in fact, they have espoused a Zapatista-style non-authoritarian socialism — and are actually fighting ISIS with some success. They deserve support from all anarchists and socialists in the world.

In Scotland the SNP has moved to the left of Labour and has virtually taken over the whole country. People there appear to be sorry now they fell for the "Better Together" hype of English propagandists, and ever more eager to leave "Great Britain", now that it's fallen into the clutches of the Tories. A Scandinavian-style social democracy in Scotland is not unimaginable. I believe anarchists should support Scottish independence — on the understanding that a free socialist Scotland would prove fertile ground for anarchist ideas. Like Connolly in Ireland in1916, I believe freedom from Imperial colonialism must precede all organization of the Social — *sine qua non.*

Therefore — I must denounce "Celtoscepticism" as a crypto-ideological ploy — apparently radical and progressive but inwardly reactionary and authoritarian. The denial of all difference in the name of a pseudo-egalitarian soup of extinguished "identities and essences" seems to me a feeble excuse for more bourgeois sameness, technopathocracy, global homogenization, anthropocene pollution of reality, boredom and disgust.

Have I resurrected in this little rant the dread specter of Romanticism? Ghosts of Shelley in Ireland? and Blake the Druid? Then so be it. I accept my fate.

The Obelisk

1. Dans la merde

No systematic ideation seems able to measure the universe — a one-to-one map even of the subjective world can probably only be achieved in non-ideational states. Nothing can be posited — "nevertheless, it moves". Something comes into cognition, and consciousness attempts to structure it. This structure is then taken for the bedrock of reality, and applied as a *mappa mundi* — first as language, then as ideology inherent in language. These language/ideology complexes tend to become orthodoxies. For example, since the Enlightenment it has been considered indisputable that only one mode of consciousness is fully real; we might call it the consciousness that "falsifies" — i.e., that verifies science as true. Before the Enlightenment other orthodoxies held sway and valued other forms of consciousness or cognition. We could sum up these earlier orthodoxies under the rubrics of God and Nature, and perhaps associate them with the Neolithic and Paleolithic, respectively. Although these worldviews retain some adherents they have been archæologically submerged, so to speak, by "Universal Reason". The Enlightenment coincides with the first determined breakthrough into scientific instrumentality and the "conquest of Nature"; God survives the onslaught for another century but finally (after a deathbed scene of positively operatic length) succumbs around 1899. Nature is silent; God is dead. Ideology is rational and scientific; the dark ages are over. If we can say that the 18th century brought us the betrayal of Nature, and the 19th century the betrayal of God, then the 20th century has certainly produced the betrayal of (and by) ideology. Enlightenment Rationalism and its offshoot/rival Dialectical Materialism have expired and gone to heaven and left us "dans la merde" (as the dying Gurdjieff told his disciples), stuck in the mire of a material world reduced to the cruel abstraction of exchange and dedicated only to its own self-defacement and disappearance.

The fact is that any map will fit any territory . . . given sufficient violence. Every ideology is complicit with every other ideology — given enough time (and rope). These complexes are nothing but unreal estate, properties to be stripped of assets, vampirized for imagery, propped up to keep the marks in line, manipulated for profit — but not taken seriously by grown-ups. For the adult of the species there remains nothing but the atomized self of exchange, and the unlikely consolations of greed and power.

2. Hermes Revividus

But there appear to exist other consciousnesses, and perhaps even kinds of cognition that remain uninvolved in consciousness in any ordinary sense. Aside from all scientific or religious definitions of these other forms, they persist in appearing, and are therefore potentially interesting. Without ideologizing these forms, can we still say anything useful about them? Language is still traditionally deemed ineffective in this regard. But *theoria,* originally in the sense of "vision" or insight, possesses a sudden and drifting nature, akin to poetry. In such terms could we speak of a kind of hermetic criticism (on the model of Dali's "paranoia criticism") capable of dealing with these other forms, however obliquely and glancingly?

It is Hermes who bridges the gap between the metalinguistic and the sublinguistic in the form of the message, language itself, the medium; he is the trickster who leads in misleading, the *tremendum* that echoes through the broken word. Hermes is therefore political, or rather ambassadorial — patron of intelligence and cryptography as well as an alchemy that seeks only the embodiment of the real. Hermes moves between text and image, master of the hieroglyphs that are simultaneously both — Hermes is their significance, their translatability. As one who goes "up and down" between spirits and humans, Hermes Psychopomp is the shamanic consciousness, the medium of direct experience, and the interface between these other forms and the political. "Hermetic" can also mean "unseen".

The late Ioan Couliano pointed out that Renaissance Hermeticism offered, as one definition of magic, the influence of text/image complexes "at a distance" on the conscious and unconscious cognition of subjects.[1] In a positive sense these techniques were meant for the "divinizing" of the magus and of material creation itself; thus alchemy is seen as a freeing of consciousness (as well as matter) from the heavier and more negative forms and its realization as self-illumination. But as Blake — himself a great hermeticist — pointed out, everything has its "form [emanation] and spectre", its positive and negative appearance. If we look at the positive "form" [emanation] of hermeticism we see it as liberation and therefore as politically radical (as with Blake, for instance); if we regard its "spectre", however, we see that the Renaissance magi were the first modern spies and the direct ancestors of all spin-doctors, PR men, advertisers and brainwashers. Or indeed— modern occultists as fascist authoritarians, ideologues of delusions, popular fads. "Hermetic criticism" as I see it would involve an attempt to "separate out" various formal [emanational] and spectral aspects of communication theory and its modern applications; but this realm is choked with undergrowth and clear separations can rarely be defended. Let's just say we're looking for patches of sunlight.

3. Critique of the Image

The critique of the Image is at the same time a defense of the Imagination.

If the spectral hermeticism of the totality consists of the totality of its imagery, then clearly something can be said in defense of iconoclasm, and for resistance to the screen (the media interface). The perfection of exchange is presented as a universal imaginaire, as a complex of images (and text/image complexes) arranged through reproduction, education, work, leisure, advertising, news, medicine, death, etc., into an apparent consensus or "totality". The unmediated is the unimagined — even though it is life itself we're discussing, we have failed to imagine it, or to evaluate it. That

---

1 Ioan P. Couliano, *Eros and Magic in the Renaissance*, Chicago: University of Chicago Press, 1987

which is present but remains unrepresented also remains virtually unreal for us, inasmuch as we have capitulated to the consensus. And since consciousness actually plays a rather miniscule role here, we all capitulate at least most of the time, either because we can't stand too much reality, or because we've decided to think about it later, or because we're afraid we're insane, and so on.

Byzantine Iconoclasm and Islam attempted to cut through the hermetic dilemma by "prohibiting" the Image. To a certain extent the latter succeeded, so that even its representational art deliberately refused perspective and dimensional illusion; moreover, in a way that Benjamin might have noticed, the painting never stands alone but is "alienated" by text that enters it and flattens it yet more. The "highest" arts are architecture as arrangement of organic space and calligraphy as arrangement of organic time; moreover the word is ideological for Islam — it not only represents logos but presents it as linearity, as a linked series of moments of meaning. Islam is "text-based" but it refuses the Image not simply to exalt the text. There are two "Korans" in Islam, and the other one is generally interpreted as integral with Nature itself as a kind of non-verbal semiotics, "waymarks on the horizon". Hence the geomorphism of the architecture, and its interaction with water, greenery, landscape and horizon — and also its ideal interpenetration by calligraphic text.

Now admittedly this ideational or religious complex can assume its own intense rigidity and heaviness; it too has its spectre. Its truly luminous organicity can perhaps best be appreciated in old anonymous unofficial forms like the domed caravansaries of Central Asia or the African mud mosques rather than in the grand imperial Masterpieces — or the catastrophic modern capital cities of Islamdom. But wherever the Image has been lost and forgotten (or at least supplanted to some extent by other possibilities) it is possible to feel in Islamic architecture a certain lightness or relief from the burden of the image, and a certain lightness in the sense of luminousness as well. Even in modern Libya under Qaddafi, which banned all commercial advertising (and allowed signs only in Arabic), one could experience at least a moment of the utopia of the absence of the image, the public image, the hieroglyphics of exchange, the iconolatry of representation. One can reject the authoritarianism of the ban on imagery without necessarily rejecting its intentionality. We could interpret it in a Sufiistic manner — that a voluntary self-restraint vis-à-vis imagery and representation (a sublimation of the image) can result in a flow of power to the autonomous ("divinized") imagination. This could also be envisioned as a suppression-and-realization in the dialectical sense. The purpose of such an exercise, from a Sufi perspective, would be to channelize the "creative imagination" toward the realization of spiritual insight — for example, revealed or inspired texts are not merely read but re-created within the imaginal consciousness. Clearly this direct experience aspect of imaginal work may raise the question of one's relation with orthodoxy and mediated spiritual authority. In some cases values are not merely re-created, but created. Values are imagined. The possibility appears that orthodoxy may deconstruct itself, that ideology may be overcome from within. Hence the ambiguous relation between Islamic authorities and Islamic mystics.[2]

The Sufi critique of the Image can certainly be "'secularized" to the extent of adding to our own concept of hermetic criticism. (Some Sufis were themselves hermeticists and even accepted the existence of Hermes Trismegistus as a "prophet".) In other words, we do not oppose the Image as theological iconoclasts but because we require the liberation of the imagination itself — our imagination, not the mediated imaginaire of the market.

Of course this critique of the image could just as well be applied to the word — to the book — to language itself. And of course it should be so applied. To question a medium is not necessarily to destroy it, in the name of either orthodoxy or heresy. The Renaissance magi were not interested merely in reading the hieroglyphs but in writing them. Hieroglyphics was seen as a kind of projective semiotics or textual imaginal performance produced to effect change in the world. The point is that we imagine ourselves rather than allow ourselves to be imagined; we must ourselves write ourselves — or else be written, to paraphrase Blake on "Systems".

2 Or so it seemed when I wrote this, before the ghastly apotheosis of Wahhabi/ Salafi puritanism and bigotry which has succeeded in ruining — perhaps forever — so many aspects of traditional Islam, notably in Æsthetics. (Added in 2018)

4. The Unseen Obelisk

If oppression emanates from the power of that which is seen, then logic might compel us to investigate the possibility that resistance could ally itself with the power of that which is unseen. The unseen is not necessarily the invisible or the disappeared. It can be seen and might be seen. It is not yet seen — or it is deliberately hidden. It reserves the right to re-appear, or to escape from representation. This hermetic ambiguity shapes its tactical movement; to use a military metaphor, it practices guerrilla techniques of "primitive war" against those of "classical war", refusing confrontation on unequal terms, melting into the generalized resistance of the excluded, occupying cracks in the strategic monolith of control, refusing the monopoly of violence to power, etc. ("Violence" here also signifies imagistic or conceptual violence.) In effect it opposes strategy (ideology) with tactics that cannot be strategically bound or ideologically fixed. It might be said that consciousness "alone" does not play as vital a role in this as certain other factors ("Freedom is a psycho-kinetic skill").

For example, there is an aspect of the unseen that involves no effort, but consists simply in the experience of places that remain unknown, times that are not marked. The Japanese æsthetic term *"wabi"* refers to the power of such places or objects — it means "poor". It is used to refer, for example, to certain teacups that appear badly-made (irregular, unevenly fired, etc.), but upon a more sensitive appraisal are seen to possess great expressiveness of "suchness" — an elegance that approaches conceptual silence — something of the melancholy of transitoriness, anonymity, a point at which poverty cannot be distinguished from the most refined æsthetic, a quintessence of the Taoist yin, the "mysterious power" of flowing water or empty space. Some of these teacups sell for millions. Most of them are made by Zen artisans who have achieved the state of wabi, but it might be said that the most prized of all would be made unselfconsciously (or even "unconsciously") by genuinely poor craftsmen. This mania for the natural and spontaneous also finds its expression in the Taoist fondness for bizarre rocks that stimulate the imagination with convolutions and extrusions and strange imbalances. Zen gardeners prefer rocks that suggest distant mountains or islands, erasing all other images, or better yet rocks suggestive of nothing at all — non-ideational form — perfect poorness.

As soon as something is represented it becomes an image of itself, semiotically richer but existentially impoverished, alienated, drawn out of itself and extenuated — a potential commodity. The wabi of the teacups is seriously compromised by the high prices they command. To be effective (to produce "satori") the object must be experienced directly and not mediated in exchange. Perhaps the really valuable cups are not yet seen because they are overlooked. No one can even perceive them, much less their value. The sole and spontaneous exception to this general inattentiveness is . . . ourselves! — we have imagined the value of wabi for these objects, times or places — for ourselves. These are perhaps among the "small pleasures" that Nietzsche says are more important than the great ones. In some cases the melancholy aspect of these things is exacerbated by the realization that time itself has overcome ugliness and turned it into an unnoticed beauty. Certain streets in North Dublin capture this quality perfectly, as do some abandoned New Jersey industrial sites where the organic (rust, water, weeds) has sculpted old machinery into spontaneous pure form and landscape. This melancholia (which was held to be a trait or sign of creativity by the old hermeticists) approaches another æsthetic term, the Persian word *dard* — which literally means "pain", but is applied in more subtle terms to the art of direct expression of certain musicians (especially singers) in the sense of a transparent and unaffected melancholic longing for an absent transcendent or beloved. The Persian fable teaches that the pain of rejected love turns an ordinary sparrow into a nightingale. The lover is poor as the dervish is poor, because desire is that which is not fulfilled — but from this poverty there emerges an æsthetic of wealth, an overflowing, a generosity or even painful excess of meaning — under the guise of melancholy and disappointment.

Aside from the inadvertency of the unseen, there also exists a more active form, so to speak — the form of the deliberate unseen. This is part of the sphere wherein appears the consciousness of everyday life of itself and its tactical intention to enhance its own unmediated pleasures and the "Situationist" autonomy of its freedom from representation. Thus conditions are maximized for the potential emergence of "the marvelous" into the sphere of lived experience. This situation resembles that of the artist — but "art" enters this space only on condition that it refuses to mediate experience for us and instead "facilitate" it. One example would be a love affair based on an eroticism that does not appear in mediation, for which no "roles" are constructed, no commodities produced. Another example might be a spontaneous festival, or a temporary autonomous zone, or a secret society; here, "art" would regain its utility.

The Renaissance magi understood that the ancient Egyptian obelisk was a perfect hermetic form for the dissemination of their hieroglyphic projective semiotics. From the top down it represents (mathematically) a sun-beam; from the bottom up, a lingam. It broadcasts or radiates its text/image complexes therefore both to the light above consciousness itself, and to the unconscious represented by sexuality. From the emblem-books such as the great *Hypnerotomachia* of 1499 we learn that the hermetic purpose for such monuments would be to call into existence the utopia of desire and the bliss of alchemical union. But the Magi never perfected their deciphering of the hieroglyphs and their utopia remained enclosed within the hermetic landscapes of the Emblems. The notion of the power of the obelisks, however, took root in western consciousness and unconsciousness, from the Napoleonic and British appropriations in Egypt to the Masonic involvement in the Washington Monument.

By contrast to the obelisk of the State, one could imagine a genuinely hermetic obelisk inscribed with magical writing about direct experience of non-ordinary consciousness; its effectiveness would consist of the near-impossibility of its being seen; it might, for example, be sited in a remote wilderness — or in the midst of abandoned industrial decay. It might even be buried. It would be a "poor" obelisk. Rumors would circulate about it. Those who actually found it would perhaps be deeply moved by its mysteriousness and remoteness. The obelisk itself might even have vanished, and been replaced again with a beam of dusty sunlight. But the story of it might retain some power.

5. The Organic Machine

But what is revolt for? Simply to assuage the terminal resentment of the eternally disappointed and belated? Could we not simply cease our agitation and pursue that teacup or that beam of sunlight, if we cannot be satisfied with the ecstasy of the totality? Why should our hermetic critique lead us to an assertion of a dialectic of presence over exchange, over alienation, over separation? If we pretend to "create values" then we should be prepared to articulate them, however much we may reject "ideology". After all, pancapitalism also rejects ideology and has even proclaimed the end of the dialectic — are our values therefore to be subsumed in Capital? If so, then — why struggle?

One possible response to this question could be made on the basis of an existentialist revolt-for-revolt's sake, in the tradition of Camus or the Italian Stirnerite anarchists. We would be ill-advised to despise this answer — but it may perhaps be possible to add to it in more positive terms (in terms of "form" [emanation], not "spectre").

For example, we could say that the Paleolithic economy of the Gift still persists, along with the "direct experience" spirituality of shamanism, and the non-separation of "Society Against the State" (Pierre Clastres), in the form of those rights and customs discussed by E. P. Thompson[3], reflected in myth and folklore, and expressed in popular festal and heretically resistant forms throughout history.[4] In other words: a tradition of resistance has persisted since the Neolithic, unbroken by the rise of the first States, and even till today. Thus: we resist and revolt because it is our glorious

---

3 E.P. Thompson, *Customs in Common: Studies in Traditional Popular Culture*, London: Merlin Press, 1991.

4 Refer to Bakhtin's *Rabelais*, to Christopher Hill's *World Turn'd Upside Down*, or Vaneigem's *Free Spirit*.

heritage to do so — it is our "conservatism". This resistance movement has become incredibly shabby and dusty since it first arose some 12,000 years ago in response to the "first ideologies" (agriculture, the calendar, the appropriation of labor) —but it still persists because it still defines most of the "empirical freedoms" that most people would like to enjoy: absence of oppression, peace, plenty, autonomy, conviviality or community, no rich or poor, spiritual expression and the pleasure of the body, and so on. It may be impossible to construct a system or ideology or strategy on such uncategorizable desires — but it is equally impossible to refute them with ideology, precisely because of their empirical and "tactical" nature. No matter what, they persist — even if they remain for all practical purposes unseen, still they refuse to go away. When all the ideas have betrayed us, this "organic machine" (Society vs. the State) declines even to define itself as an idea. It remains loyal to our immemorial inarticulacy, our silence, our poorness.

Capital pursues its telos beyond the human. Science has already betrayed us — perhaps the next (or last) betrayal will be of the human itself, and of the entire material world. Only two examples need be given here to illuminate (rather than "prove") this contention. The first concerns money, which in the last few decades has transcended its links with production to the alarming degree that some 94.2% of the global "money supply" now consists of pure financial capital. I've called this the Gnostic uploading of the economic body, in honor of those old Gnostic Dualists and their hatred of everything material. The practical result of this situation is staggering for any consideration of economic justice as an "empirical" concern, since the migratory or nomadic nature of pancapitalism permits "disembodied Capital" to strip the productive economy of its assets in the cause of profits that can only be measured by purely "spiritual" means. Moreover, this Capital has become its own medium, and now attempts to define a universal discourse in which alternatives to exchange simply vanish as if they'd never existed and could never exist. Thus all human relations are to be measured in money.

To illustrate Capital as its own medium, and as our second

example, we can look at bioengineering. There is no force that can prevent pancapitalism from acquiring patents to every identifiable gene. This means that farmers are now being asked to pay "rents" on certain genetic strains that they themselves developed, because the "rights" to those strains were acquired by the mega-corporations. The dubious triumph of cloning is supposed to compensate for the profit-driven ravaging of Nature's last remnants. Moreover, the human genome project, which has "solved" the production of life as a biochemical machine, allows "evolution" itself to be coopted and absorbed into Capital. As the market envisions the future, the human itself will become humanity's final commodity — and into this "value" the human will disappear. Capital's self-defacement implies humanity's self-effacement. Acting as a purely spiritual substance — money — Capital will attain the ownership of life's becoming, and thus the power to shape the very protoplasm of the material world as pure exchange.

Our essential question then concerns the possibility of the re-appearance of the unseen as opposition. Finally it would seem that a tactical refusal of all strategic systemization may be inadequate to bring about this desired re-appearance. A positive proposal is required to balance the gestures of refusal. We must hope that an organic strategy of victory will emerge as "spontaneous ordering" from the driftwork of tactics. Any attempt to impose this strategic unity from "above" must be renounced as (at best) nostalgia for the lost utopia of ideology — or as "bad religion" of some sort.

But just as the Image has its spectre and its form [emanation], so we might play with the notion that the Idea, too, has a spectral and a formal [emanational] manifestation. As a "spook in the head" the idea remains nothing but a semantic trap — disguised for example as a moral imperative. But as a "form" [emanation] in the Blakean sense the idea itself may take on organicity as a production of the body and the "creative intellect", just as the image may be turned toward realization by the body and the "creative imagination". Perhaps in some sense it is the idea that has remained unseen till now, and thus retains all its power, having never fallen away into representation. Neglected all along — having never been given a price — and perhaps remaining inexpressible even in its manifestation — this idea may "give meaning to revolt". And it may be written ambiguously in hieroglyphs whose meaning is uncertain, but whose "magical" effect is nevertheless potent — it may be written even on a hidden obelisk. But it will have been written by us.

6. Platonic Nets

It seems as if there should exist two possible kinds of network (or even of communication technology) — one Aristotelian, text-based, linear — the other Platonic, image-based, non-linear. Language, for example, as viewed from this perspective might appear more Platonic, since words are based on "inner pictures" and thus cannot be limited by pure lexicality or one-to-one "translation"; while by contrast a network of computers, using digital text-based programming, might appear as a perfect Aristotelian system.

But this neat dualism dissolves into paradox and conundrum. Text itself is picture-based (hence "non-linear") in Sumer, Egypt, China. Even our alphabet is picture-based; the letter "p", for example, is simply an upside-down foot, since Indo-European words for "foot" almost always begin with "p" (or "f"). Text, which is supposed to be linear, is "language-based" and partakes of language's non-linearity. When "speech genres" are textualized they become in some senses more linear (because stripped of contextual depth formerly provided by the extra dimensions of speech such as tone, gesture, performance, etc.) — but in some other ways this stripping of language to produce text results in further ambiguities, since the context of the text now consists largely of the reader and the reader's inner world.

Thus the fact that computers are digital (simple on/off switches in massive array) and text-based does not make them genuine Aristotelian machines, since image is already embedded in language, and even more because the screen itself is also already an image, whether it displays image, text, or both at once. If programming could be based directly on images rather than text — as some savants believe possible — the computer could easily be seen as a

Platonic machine. The Platonizing effect of the computer is already present not only in its screenal display of images but also in the psychological reality of the screen as image. In effect, the computer is a hieroglyphic machine, an interface mode of text and image; hence its magic appearance to the unconscious. In this sense, both money and "information" can be theorized as forms of *black magic* or necromancy.

The Renaissance magi (especially Athanasius Kircher) believed that the Egyptian hieroglyphs were purely Platonic — (in this, they followed Plotinus and Iamblichus) — that is, that each image was an ideal form, and that their deployment could not only indicate meaning but also create and project it. Thus the hieroglyphs were seen as an ideal amalgam of text and image — an emblematic form of writing. Now when Champollion deciphered the Rosetta Stone, it was discovered that hieroglyphs were already used quasi-alphabetically (on the model of "[picture] foot = [phoneme] p"), although there were also cases where single images or imageclusters represented the objects depicted as words. This discovery relegated the unsuccessful translation attempts of the old magi to complete oblivion. Their theories are now only mentioned in passing as examples of "false" hermetic science and bad Egyptology. But as Couliano noted, these discarded theories have great secret heuristic power, because they describe empirically some of the ways in which text, image, and mind interact. Once the neoplatonic metaphysics and crude magical fantasies have been discarded, hieroglyphic theory can be used to understand the mode of operation of text/image complexes — that is, emblems. This formula does not constitute a rejection of neoplatonism, which of course still underlies most classical occult theory, but only of a certain "Platonic dualism".

The emblem books were Renaissance experiments in the "projective semiotics" of hieroglyph-theory. Allegorical pictures accompanied by texts (often one text in prose and one in poetry) — and in a few cases even by music (the great *Atalanta fugiens* of Michael Maier, for example) — were collected in sequences, published as books, and intended for the magical edification of readers. The "morals" of the emblems were thus conveyed on more than one level at once. Each emblem was simultaneously:

a) a picture accompanied by words;

b) a picture "translated" from words. That is, the pictures' real values are not purely formal but also allegorical, so that Hercules stands for "strength", Cupid for "desire", and the emblem itself can be read as a "sentence" composed of these "words";

c) a hieroglyphic "coding" in which certain images not only represent words but also "express the essence" of those words, and project them in a "magical" manner, whether or not the reader is consciously aware of this process; thus graphic qualities, not only verbal meanings, contribute to an emblem's sense.

Our working hypothesis is that the world's image of itself not only defines its possibilities but also its limits. The world's representation of itself to itself (its "macrocosmic" image) is no more and no less than the self's "microcosmic" image of itself "writ large" so to speak, on the level of *mentalité* and the *imaginaire*. This is part of our "secularized" hermetic theory; it explains, for instance, why emblems have influences on multiple levels of cognition.

The radical magi encountered a world wherein one world-image was locked in place — not just the geocentric cosmos but the whole Christian orthodox value system that went with it. Their subversive purpose revolved around the project of a free circulation of imagery, a breaking-up of the stasis and the creation of a more responsive model. The single world-view of orthodoxy was seen as stifling, tyrannical, oppressive. Inasmuch as they self-interiorized this view it reproduced the oppression on the level of the subjective. The hermeticists opposed the very singleness of this worldview with a contradictory multiplicity, a critical form of "paganism" based on difference.

Analogously, since 1989-91 we have entered a new "dark age" in which one worldview (and its imaginaire) claims hegemony over all difference. Not only is "pancapitalism" a global system, it has also become its own medium, so to speak, in that it proposes a universal stasis of imagery. The free circulation of the image is blocked when one image of the world structures the world's self-image. In turn this image rests, so to speak, in the totalitarian monopoly of infinite imagery that constitutes "information ontology". To every man and every micro-sub-moiety its own image stash but in such a way that the correspondence between micro and macro worlds — here understood as private and public — is interrupted. True difference is leached away toward disappearance and replaced by an obsessive re-cycling and sifting-through of "permitted" imagery within the single system of discourse (like the medieval theologians who supposedly quarreled over the gender of angels as the Turks besieged Byzantium). Pancapitalism "permits" any imagery that enhances profit — hence in theory it might permit any imagery — but in practice, it cannot. This is the crisis of "postmodernism" — crisis as a form of stasis, of infinite re-circulation of the same — the impossibility of difference.

Within the crisis of stasis all manner of imagery can be allowed or even encouraged when it tends toward the depiction of relation as exchange — even the imagery of terror, murder, crime — even the extinction of Nature and the Human — all this can be turned (as imagery at least) into profit. What cannot be allowed (except perhaps as nostalgia) is the imagery of relations other than exchange. Nostalgia can be contained and marketed — but actual difference would threaten the hegemony of the one worldview. The "Gift Economy" of some nearly-extinguished "primitive tribe" makes excellent TV; our mourning for its disappearance can only boost the sales of whatever commodity might soothe our sense of loss. Mourning itself can become fetishized, as in the Victorian era of onyx and jet and black-plumed graveyard horses. Death is good for Capital, because money is the sexuality of the dead. Corpses have already appeared in advertising — "real" corpses.

Assuming that our hypothesis holds so far, we might well ask from "whence" there could appear any image of true difference in such a situation. The obvious answer is that it would have to come from "outside" the stasis.

This means war, obviously. At the very least, it means

"Image War".

But how can we even begin to define what might lie "outside" the stasis? Are we not precisely engaged in a situation where all circulating images become part of the crisis of circulation? This is the "malign hermeticism" of the totality of mediation — its spectral metastasis, so to speak — ontology as oncology. Everything that enters the discourse, all that which is "seen", is subverted by the very fact that there is only one discourse, one exchange. "Image War" might be just as productive for exchange as other forms of "pure war", since it would at least offer an "illusion of choice". This, then, is the hermetic crisis of the tactical media.

7. Tactical Media

The unseen lies at least potentially outside the space of the represented totality. Thus it becomes for tactical media a subject of great theoretical interest. But as media the tactical media must still mediate, and therefore the unseen remains "mysterious" in the precise sense of the term. Since only the seen can be described, the pure unseen cannot be written about or represented — although it can be communicated, at least in "Zen" terms.

However the unseen is not necessarily "pure". If it were pure, it would interest us a great deal less than it does, since it would thereby share in a characteristic we associate with ideology and stasis. In fact the unseen attracts us because of its impurity.

In effect there appear to exist degrees of the unseen. The unseen can paradoxically appear even within the locked circularity of the mediated totality, either inadvertently or else by subversion. For example the TV show about the primitive tribe, and the melancholy of the disappearance of the Gift, cannot touch the unseen actuality of the Gift and its meaning for the people who know it. But sometimes the spoken text or the editing of the film will create potent cognitive dissonances with certain images that suggest the presence of the unseen, at least for a few viewers who are prepared for such irruptions of the mysterious, its "guerrilla" raids on consensus consciousness.

Moreover, the "intimate media" remain relatively invisible

to the totality because they are so "poor". The petty extent to which such media participate in market economics, much less consensus æsthetics, makes them so insignificant as to render them meaningless for all practical purposes. Of course as soon as any energy and originality is seen to emanate from such media they are at once absorbed into Capital — and the unseen must retreat, drift on, evade definition, move elsewhere. But this process takes time, and time makes opportunities.

Thus tactical media could make use either of "guerrilla" operations within the media totality, or of intimate media that remain (in some impure manner) outside that totality. But in either case tactical integrity would demand that such "appearances" take place only where they can be effective — in military terms: where they can damage the totality without being absorbed into its "spectacle of dissidence" and permitted rebelliousness. Tactical media will retreat from any such englobement, and in such moments of tactical withdrawal tactical media may have to engage in violence and sacrifice (at least on a conceptual level). Tactical media will make mistakes — all the more so because of its improvisational nature, the absence of any overall strategy. Because tactical media refuses purity, it will engage — and it will be defeated, very often by its own "success".

The purpose and intention of tactical media is precisely not to rejuvenate the consensus by allowing itself to be vampirized of its creative energies by the imaginaire of the Undead and its "natural laws" of exchange. But we cannot say therefore that the purpose of tactical media "is" the destruction of the totality. This statement of identity would define an ideology or source of authority for tactical media, and limit it to the role of opposition —in effect, to its "spectral" appearance. We certainly don't wish long life and success to the totality, but by defining ourselves (or our techniques) solely as "destructive" we are simply inviting our own recuperation into the pattern of oppression. Tactical media, I suggest, should be about something and for something — this would constitute its "formal" (emanational) appearance. It should be for the unseen — even for a seduction into the unseen.

Does this mean that the tactics of tactical media can only be defined "situationally"? Even if we reject all ideologizing of   intentionality can we still say anything descriptive about specific goals? If we refuse strategy, can we nevertheless articulate something about a tendency or movement or unifying imaginaire of presence (a "myth" perhaps) that might underlie and inform our tactical mediations?

This may indeed be possible, if only because the imaginal values in the process of emergence in tactical media seem to concern those empirical freedoms expressed not only in immemorial "rights and customs" but also in the most radical politics of desire. In other words, an "organic" substitute for strategy/ideology arises from a shared imaginaire based on such traditional yet radical perspectives. It is in this way that tactical media can be seen as an aspect of a possible effective opposition to exchange itself, to the post ideological ideology of Capital — an opposition that cannot be englobed, and therefore can contemplate the possibility of victory.

All this is pure hypothesis, so it would be pointless and perhaps even counter-productive to engage in any attempt to prescribe or predict or even to influence the tactical media. The historical movement envisioned here (which even faces the challenge of the very "End of History") can make nothing out of any outmoded vanguardism or "unacknowledged legislator"-ism of a discredited intelligentsia, artists, etc., etc. It does, however, seem possible to adopt an "experimental" approach. Who can foretell success or failure? An inherent weakness for narrativity, however, and a desire to work on some sort of "emblematic" structure leads me to an "aimless wandering" or Taoist theorizing around certain themes considered here — notably the notions of hermeticism in both its "formal" (emanational) and "spectral" aspects. For instance: since money is "imaginal" it is susceptible to hermetic manipulation. It seems theoretically possible to "hack" money at the level of its representationality — all the more so now that most of it is pure representation. Money that can be manipulated imagistically because money itself is image, however, can also be "downloaded" from its CyberGnostic numisphere and manifested on the earthly plane as hard cash, goods, production. Thus it would appear feasible to redirect capital as wealth, away from areas where pancapitalism has "decreed" its (symbolic) presence, into areas where it has "forbidden" its (real) presence.

"Decree" and "forbid" are enclosed by quotation marks because in truth the situation is so complex that "legality" has become an extremely ambiguous category. Money as medium is engulfed in the same crisis of definition as all the other media. Into this space of uncertainty, hermetic operations could be directed (in perfectly legal ways) such as to interfere with the circulation of Capital. The space of uncertainty — the crack in the monolith of representation — has its deep origin in the intense anxiety of the crisis of stasis. The image of the imaginaire as a labyrinth with no exit induces a kind of claustrophobia akin to that experienced by the Renaissance occultists in relation to the cosmic stasis of doctrine: escape panic. We are after all still "in transition" toward a perfect global market — the cosmos of economy is not yet fully and flawlessly enclosed.[5]

Hence for instance the sudden obsession with "content". What are we going to do with all the data — what use is it? And who shall create in order that others (all others) may consume? A real puzzle.

Certain elements within political structures still retain a half -hearted sentimentality about the "Social" state; they still want to help program the "content". They are opposed by the mega-corporations that demand "pure" content, measurable only by price rather than value. But what do "the people" want? Into the tactical spaces left vacant by this clash of bewildered titans, certain mediations might be effected. The old magic power of the scribe, the hermetic initiate, might constitute a counter-force to the magic power of the manipulation of content, the monopoly of meaning and interpretation claimed by the totality (which suddenly doesn't

---

5 When I wrote this the full extent of new media and representation had not yet manifested, not to mention the zombie culture of pure information, or virtual money, or the almost certain extinction of Civilization through its own shit. I'm less "anti-pessimistic" now. (2018)

look quite so total . . .).

As we are discussing media, the evocation of the word "magic" seems somehow permissible. How relevant these musings might prove to situations encountered in unmediated reality — perhaps that is another kettle of fish. For now, however, we are simply exercising our imagination.

NYC
May 1, 1997

2018 Comment: Over twenty years ago it still seemed possible to view "tactical media" as a potential "virus" that might infect the Totality and help dissolve its power. By now, with the global triumph of "social media" and its virulent erasure of both the individual and the Social, my old ideas appear naïve indeed. Nevertheless I won't repudiate this text entirely. It could happen that a new generation may grow tired of having to pay to be sick. The repressed might return again. Or maybe not.

About the Author

Peter Lamborn Wilson has published (as author, co-translator, editor, etc.) over sixty books and countless articles. Works have been translated into Dutch, German, Swedish, French, Italian, Spanish, Portuguese, Gallego, Arabic, Slovenian, Bengali, Hungarian, Québécois, Japanese, Czech, & Turkish. He lives in the Hudson Valley. He was born in another century.

COLOPHON

The New Nihilism was published in August 2018 by Bottle of Smoke Press. Designed and typeset by Bill Roberts in North Salem, NY. The text is set in Adobe Caslon Pro.

Made in the USA
Middletown, DE
26 June 2021

liked one of her videos before, at least not officially. He felt his face growing warm, hot even, as he summoned the courage to click. His eyes swam in and out of focus from the blond preacher to the clock in the corner of his screen. Yipes! It was time to go. He depressed the mouse button and, before he could see what happened, slammed the laptop shut. He let out a deep breath and placed the computer back on its shelf, his limbs tingly and a little wobbly.

"C'mon, Timothy," he said to himself. "Time to go to work. You don't want to disappoint Mr. Spooner."

Tim's boss was just about the coolest guy there was. Maybe sometimes he could be a little mean, but that's just how cool guys were. To be cool, you had to be a little mean. Tim gave the apartment a once-over, to make sure everything was in order. He straightened the dish towel and made sure the chairs were square to the table. He looked at the digital clock on the stove.

"Jeepers! It's really time to go!"

Tim grabbed his keys, his coat, and his umbrella, just in case. It looked nice out, but Tim liked to be prepared. It turned out that he needed neither coat nor umbrella. It was a beautiful day. The bus arrived at the bus stop at the same time that Tim did. It was like Sandy Newman had said. It was a blessed day. A *most* blessed day. The bus hummed down the twelve stops without incident, and Tim got off. He smiled and whistled to himself as he walked across the vast expanse of blacktop that separated the SuperMart from the road. There was room for so many cars. He looked up at the sign. Tiny red lettering said WELCOME TO, and beneath that, huge blue letters on a white background shouted MEGA SUPERMART.

Tim straightened up a little bit. They had just become a Mega SuperMart last year. It was a big deal. There were only seven in the whole country. And theirs was the closest to the SuperGroup headquarters. It wasn't an official title, but Tim liked to think of it as sort of the flagship. Sure, SuperMart was more of a regional chain, but it was up and coming, and being a Mega SuperMart

was a mega super big deal; they had just about everything to be
a one-stop shop for their customers. Groceries, home and bath,
home and garden, toys, automotive supplies, sporting goods—
they even had a café at the front of the store where people could
take a break from all their shopping. Top-notch coffee, pastries,
a selection of soups and sandwiches, even salads for the health-
conscious types. The café was delicious. Like everything else in
the store, the food was tip-top quality and available for the best
prices. The store sure was a pretty great place, and Tim knew it
better than anyone, except maybe for Mr. Spooner. Tim knew
where everything belonged, so he could always help a customer
find just what he or she needed. And he ate lunch at the café
almost every day, so he could recommend just the right item on
the menu to satisfy any appetite. Yep, the store needed all that
space for parking. He had never seen it actually full, but he was
glad to know it was there, just in case.

Right now, though, the parking lot was empty. Almost empty.
There was a Ford Taurus sitting way over by the Coffee Xpress
in the far corner of the parking lot. Tim wasn't sure if they
had a deal with Coffee Xpress for the parking lot. He thought
maybe they did. Except wasn't the Coffee Xpress vacant? He'd
have to check sometime. If someone was parking in the parking
lot without permission, well, that was against the rules. But if
it was, then he might have to do something about it. And Tim
hated conflict. It was a tough one. Maybe he could wait to check
about whether they had a parking lot–sharing agreement with
Coffee Xpress. Besides, he had work to do.

He had arrived right on time, an hour before doors opened.
He'd have just enough time to get the coffee going and plug in
the various peripherals in the executive suite he shared with Mr.
Spooner. If he really hustled, he might even have time to sweep
Mr. Spooner's parking spot! As the assistant manager, Tim had
the smaller office, more like a closet really, but he understood.
Mr. Spooner needed the other three offices for important store-
manager stuff. It was an honor just to be in the same space. The